Alexander the Great
AND HIS EMPIRE

Alexander the Great
AND HIS EMPIRE

A SHORT INTRODUCTION

Pierre Briant

TRANSLATED BY AMÉLIE KUHRT

PRINCETON UNIVERSITY PRESS

PRINCETON AND OXFORD

First published in France under the title *Alexandre le Grand*. Copyright ©
Presses Universitaires de France, 1974.
English translation copyright © 2010 by Princeton University Press.
Requests for permission to reproduce material from this work should be sent
to Permissions, Princeton University Press.

Published by Princeton University Press, 41 William Street,
Princeton, New Jersey 08540

In the United Kingdom: Princeton University Press, 6 Oxford Street,
Woodstock, Oxfordshire OX20 1TW

press.princeton.edu

Third printing, and first paperback printing, 2012
Paperback ISBN 978-0-691-15445-9

The Library of Congress has cataloged the cloth edition of this book as follows

Briant, Pierre.
    [Alexandre le Grand. English]
    Alexander the Great and his empire : a short introduction / Pierre Briant ;
translated by Amélie Kuhrt.
        p.   cm.
    First published under the title Alexandre le Grand. Paris : Presses
universitaires de France, 1974.
    Includes bibliographical references and index.
    ISBN 978-0-691-14194-7 (hardcover : acid-free paper)   1. Alexander,
the Great, 356–323 B.C.   2. Alexander, the Great, 356–323 B.C.—
Travel—Turkey.   3. Alexander, the Great, 356–323 B.C.—Military
leadership.   I. Title.
    DF234.37.B7413 2010
    938′.07092—dc22   2009047945

British Library Cataloging-in-Publication Data is available

This book has been composed in Goudy Oldstyle
Printed on acid-free paper. ∞

Printed in the United States of America

10 9 8 7 6 5 4 3

Contents

List of Illustrations	vii
Translator's Note	ix
Foreword to the American Edition	xi
Acknowledgments	xxi

Introduction
Alexander before the Expedition to Asia Minor (356–334)   1

**Chapter I   The Major Stages of the Conquest   7
(334–323)**

From Granicus to the Fall of Tyre (May 334–Summer 332)   7
From Tyre to the Euphrates (Summer 332–Summer 331)   10
The End of Darius and the Final Submission of Greece
     (Summer 331–Summer 330)   12
Guerillas in the Eastern Satrapies and Macedonian
     Opposition (Summer 330–Spring 327)   14
The Conquest of India and the Return via the
     Persian Gulf (327–325)   20
The Last Years (324–323)   22

**Chapter II   The Origins and Objectives of the
               Conquest   24**

The Unsatisfactory Nature of Explanations Based on
     Personality and Psychology   25
The Heritage of Philip II   28
Alexander and the Royal Territories of the Achaemenids   32
"War of Liberation" and "War of Reprisal":
     The Limits of Alexander's Philhellenism   33
The Conquest of India and Return via the Persian Gulf   37
The Problem of the "Last Plans"   38

Chapter III   Resistance to the Conquest   42

The Resistance of Darius (334–330)   42
Underground Resistance and Open Revolt in Greece   52

CONTENTS

Resistance and Reprisals in the Eastern Satrapies (330–327)   54
The Discontent of the Macedonian Soldiery (330–324)   63

Chapter IV   The Administration, Defense, and Exploitation of the Conquered Lands   67
The Different Degrees of Royal Authority   68
Territorial Control and the Management of the Population   80
Conquest and "Economic Development"   83

Chapter V   Alexander among Macedonians, Greeks, and Iranians   101
Conquest and Surrender: Contradiction and Opposition   102
A Policy for the Future (325–323)   126

Conclusion
The King Is Dead! Long Live the King?   139

An Introductory Bibliography   145
Appendix   The History of Alexander Today: A Provisional Assessment and Some Future Directions   153
Index of Toponyms   187
General Index   190

Illustrations

Maps

Map 1 Alexander's conquest: the main routes
         and battles   16–17
Map 2 Alexander's 329–27 campaigns in Bactria
         and Sogdiana   18
Map 3 Detail of Bactria and Sogdiana   19

Figures

Figure 1 Portrait of Alexander. Detail of the
           Alexander mosaic, Naples   xvi
Figure 2 Silver coin of Mazakes, satrap of Egypt   11
Figure 3 "Poros decadrachm"   22
Figure 4 Portrait of Darius. Detail of the Alexander
           mosaic, Naples   49
Figure 5 "Royal Hero" on the obverse of an
           Achaemenid silver siglos   98
Figure 6 Mazday receives Alexander at the gates
           of Babylon   106
Figure 7 The tomb of Cyrus the Great   112
Figure 8 Royal audience, relief panel from
           Persepolis   124
Figure 9 Hunt scene on the Alexander
           Sarcophagus   133

Figure 10 "Alexander Medallion" and coin
showing Alexander with an elephant's
scalp on his head   164–65
Figure 11 "Persian Hero," from a Samarian
seal impression   177

Translator's Note

Publications frequently referred to in the footnotes are cited in abbreviated form as follows:

Bosworth, *Alexander and the East* = A. B. Bosworth, *Alexander and the East: The Tragedy of Triumph*, Oxford 1996.

Bosworth, *Commentary* = A. B. Bosworth, *A Historical Commentary on Arrian's History of Alexander* I–II, Oxford 1980, 1995.

Bosworth, *Conquest and Empire* = A. B. Bosworth, *Conquest and Empire: The Reign of Alexander the Great*, Oxford 1988.

Briant, *Antigone* = P. Briant, *Antigone le Borgne: les débuts de sa carrière et les problèmes de l'assemblée macédonienne* (Centre de Recherches d'Histoire Ancienne 10), Paris 1973.

Briant, *L'Asie Centrale* = *L'Asie centrale et les royaumes proche-orientaux du premier millénaire (c. VIIIe–IVe siècle av.n.è.)* (Recherches sur les Civilisations 42), Paris 1984.

Briant, *Darius dans l'ombre* = P. Briant, *Darius dans l'ombre d'Alexandre*, Paris 2003.

Briant, *États et pasteurs* = P. Briant, *États et pasteurs au Moyen-Orient ancien*, Paris and Cambridge 1982.

Briant, *History* = P. Briant, *From Cyrus to Alexander: History of the Persian Empire* (English translation of *Histoire de l'empire perse: de Cyrus à Alexandre*, Paris 1996), Winona Lake, IN 2002.

Briant, *Rois, tributs et paysans* = P. Briant, *Rois, tributs et paysans: études sur les formations tributaires au Moyen-Orient ancien* (Centre de Recherches d'Histoire Ancienne 43), Paris 1982.

Briant-Joannès, eds, *La Transition* = P. Briant & F. Joannès, eds., *La transition entre l'empire achéménide et les royaumes hellénistiques* (Persika 9), Paris 2006.

Le Rider, *Alexander the Great* = G. Le Rider, *Alexander the Great. Coinage, Finances and Policy* (trans.), Philadelphia 2007.

For a list of further relevant abbreviations, see either Briant, *History* (2002) or A. Kuhrt, *The Persian Empire: A Corpus of Sources* (2 vols.), London 2007.

All references to Arrian are to Arrian's *Anabasis of Alexander*, unless otherwise stated.

I should like to thank Dr. Robert Allen for his editorial help, which has improved the English of the translation.

A. K.

Foreword to the American Edition

The first edition of this book was published in 1974 in Paris by the Presses Universitaires de France in its well-known series *Que-sais-je?* (no. 622), replacing an earlier book with the same title by Paul Cloché, which had appeared in 1954. Since then there have been five new French editions (published between 1976 and 2005), as well as translations into several European languages (Italian, Danish, Swedish, Bulgarian-Macedonian, Romanian, Greek, Portuguese-Brazilian), as well as Chinese and Japanese.

In terms of structure and basic ideas, the present book is very similar to the one published in French in 1974. I remain committed to the agenda with which I prefaced the first edition:

> This is not a biography. Its aim is rather to consider major aspects of a historical phenomenon that is not reducible merely to the person of Alexander, however important the role played by that personal element may have been. The book's structure reflects that deliberate choice. The account of Alexander's conquest itself is concentrated in a short preliminary chapter, to familiarize the reader with its chronology. The main body of the book is devoted to examining the larger questions it raises: the origins of the conquest and Alexander's aims; the nature and relative importance of various forms of resistance encountered; the organization of the conquered territories; and relations between conquerors and conquered.

Nevertheless, while keeping the same approach, I have updated the text as appropriate for each edition. I have taken care to rewrite sections where my presentation no longer seemed appropriate in the light of new documents and associated interpretations, but also as a result of changes in my own ideas on the subject.

The present edition has, furthermore, been revised with close attention to each page. Several discussions have been completely recast. New maps and several illustrations have been added. As the format envisaged by Princeton University Press allows me more flexibility than did that of the French publication, I have been able to include many more references both to ancient texts as well as recent studies. I have not tried to add exhaustive bibliographic references, as I feel they would be as likely to confuse as to enlighten. In order to widen the perspective, I thought it would be useful to add a section specifically devoted to bibliographical and historiographical issues. This is contained in the appendix and will, I hope, complement the main body of the book.[1]

Fairly simple considerations have determined the successive rewritings of the text. I tried to explain the reasons in an introductory note added to the French editions of 1994, 2002, and 2005:

> Just as in other fields of the social sciences, the history of the ancient world is not based on unassailable certainties. Each year a large number of publications appear, which add to the issues and serve to reopen questions regarding the history of Alexander. These owe less to the appearance of new documents (which are unfortunately rare for this period), than to the current revival of research into Achaemenid history.

---

[1] See the appendix, "The History of Alexander Today: A Provisional Assessment and Some Future Directions," at the end of this volume. Note in particular the bibliographical tables included in the appendix, in which each item cited is labeled with both a letter (A or B) and a number (A1, B2 and so forth). In the following pages, many articles will be referred to in this manner.

This has led to a different perception of Alexander's conquests, placing them into the context of Middle Eastern history in the first millennium BC and freeing Alexander from the Hellenocentrism which has, for too long, dominated discussions. The increasingly regular use now made of Babylonian and Egyptian documents to analyze Alexander's policy in Babylonia and Egypt and the response of local aristocracies to that policy has been one outcome of this development. Conversely, Assyriologists and Egyptologists are paying more attention to these periods, which for long were left to the expertise of "classicists."

At times scholars have wanted to see my book as "a violent attack on the Graeco-Roman or European perspective predominant in former scholarship."[2] This has never been my aim, nor is it now. Although this short book takes an unambiguous stance within current debates, it is not driven by a wish to be polemical. All I want is to introduce into discussions of the subject certain aspects that are, as a rule, not considered. In an attempt to take all the possibilities of historical enquiry into consideration, I have merely suggested shifting the vision of the single observer and replacing it with multiple points of view.

The introductory note from the first edition that I have just quoted effectively reasserts one of my objectives and starting points, namely that we should not focus too much on the personality of Alexander, and must never "forget his adversary, who is too frequently left out of the picture as though Alexander was all alone as he embarked on his personal adventure" (1974, p. 27). This explains why I included sections specifically devoted to the war as viewed from Darius's side (1974, pp. 44–53). In the 1974 edition of

[2] J. Carlsen, "Alexander the Great (1970–1990)," in B9 (1993): 64.

this book, I made an observation which, ever since, has seemed self-evident to me, namely that "it is a grave error of judgment to underestimate the Achaemenid empire's capacity for resistance and the courage of its ruler" (p. 44). The need to investigate this aspect has emerged ever more clearly as the result of the development of Achaemenid studies in the past thirty years.

This does not, of course, mean that we should simplistically reverse our point of view in order to see the conquest exclusively from the Persian perspective (as would be the temptation in a work devoted to Achaemenid history), nor should we chase some kind of illusory "victims' history." Rather, we need to interrogate both camps at one and the same time, and in turn. To state what may well seem obvious: in a conflict of such magnitude as this one the interests and reactions of the conquerors become inevitably entwined with those of the conquered peoples in all their variety and inconsistency, from the Mediterranean to the Indus, from Elephantine to Samarkand.

This book, like any other, is the product of both editorial constraints and choices made by the writer. The reader must not expect a history with a continuous narrative nor one following a clear chronological framework, with the exception of a resumé of events in the first chapter. Certain matters are not treated at all, and others only marginally or noted in passing. There is, for example, little discussion of Macedon and Greece prior to the campaigns in the Middle East and Central Asia. And while Greece and Europe figure only rarely, Darius's empire is very much present throughout. As I have explained above, the reason for this is simple: the book's organizing principle is the issue of the conquest— but not so much in military terms as in its political and organizational aspects, hence the title of the American edition. The reader will not find any technical analysis of the armies, or of weapons or tactics, let alone any discussion of the great set battles. The studies and articles on these questions are practically without number.[3] Some topics of considerable interest, which have attracted attention again recently, in particular the life inside Alexander's "itinerant kingdom," have also had to be omitted.

More surprising, perhaps, is the absence of a chapter devoted to the sources. But there is already such a plethora of studies on this subject[4] that, in the context of such a short and condensed book, I felt it unnecessary to present the material again. I am nonetheless, of course, very conscious that our knowledge of Alexander's conquests is limited and uncertain, primarily as a result of the inadequacy of the documentary corpus, both quantitatively and qualitatively.

We do not have official court archives, and Greek civic inscriptions reflect only the tiniest fraction of the archives of the cities.[5] Archaeological sources datable to Alexander's reign in the Middle East are virtually nonexistent. The two most famous iconographic documents—the Alexander Mosaic in Naples (Fig. 1) and the Alexander Sarcophagus in Istanbul (Fig. 9)—were both created after the death of Alexander, whose heroic image they portray in line with what had already become the canonical presentation.[6] The only

---

[3] See, most conveniently, W. Heckel, *The Conquests of Alexander the Great*, Cambridge 2008.

[4] All manuals and monographs contain at least one chapter on the sources; cf. recently, for example, B4 (1975): 297–300; B8 (1992): 13–152; B12 (1995): 1–24; B14 (2000): 1–17, 286–325; B15 (1998): 3–30; B17 (2003): 1–16.

[5] A listing of Greek and Macedonian epigraphic material is provided in the bibliography.

[6] See the interesting, but highly speculative, recent suggestion by W. Heckel, "Mazaeus, Callisthenes and the Alexander Sarcophagus," *Historia* 55 (2006): 385–96, that the patron was Mazday/Mazaeus, who died in 328.

Fig. 1. Portrait of Alexander. Detail of the Alexander Mosaic, ca. 100 BC, Naples National Archaeological Museum. Drawing from Niccolini, "Musaico scoperto in Pompei il di 24 ottobre 1831," *Real Museo Borbonico* 8, Naples 1832, Pl. XXXVII.

quantitatively significant source is the coinage, which has been the subject of recent and well-informed studies.[7]

Finds of new materials directly linked to the history of Alexander have been few,[8] and even those have given rise either to doubts about their authenticity or to disputes about their interpretation.[9] With documents dated to Alexander's reign, which exist in various languages, the situation is different. Such material survives from Lydia and Bactria, as well as Egypt, Idumaea, and Babylonia, and provides the opportunity to trace both administrative and political aspects of the transition from Darius's empire to that of Alexander.[10]

The surviving Graeco-Roman narrative sources in Greek

[7] See in particular Le Rider, *Alexander the Great*.

[8] For the fragment (tentatively attributed to Strattis of Olynthus) concerning Alexander's Balkan campaign, see, for example, B11 (1993, I): 27–44 (Hammond).

[9] For the "Alexander medallion," see the appendix.

[10] See the appendix.

(Diodorus, Plutarch, Arrian) or in Latin (Quintus Curtius, Justin) continue to form the core of the evidence. They were, however, composed between two and four centuries after Alexander. Moreover, not one of these ancient authors was a "historian" as we understand the term now, with respect either to method, to concept, or to procedure. Each had of course a somewhat different mode of approaching the subject, but it may be said of all of them that they were not so much "Alexander historians" as writers marked by the Roman milieu in which they were operating and, in some cases, also by their fascination with Greek "classical" culture. They were thus, first and foremost, concerned with establishing their credentials as literary figures, which demanded that they follow the literary conventions of the day. These called for imitating models from the past (*mimesis* [imitation]) and engaging in a contest (*agon* [competition]) with their literary colleagues. Their works are generally more comparable to storytelling than critical history. How to take these factors into account is the problem: "The reader is controlled by an increasingly artificial source tradition which turned the raw events of Alexander's reign into a literary construct."[11] I would add that in view of this situation it is often a matter of conjecture what "the raw events" might actually have been!

On the other hand, the aim of this book is not "to reduce this history to a literary construct," nor (obviously) to avoid trying to understand, for example, "why the Persians were defeated and why the death of Darius is synonymous with the end of the empire."[12] Nor does my statement imply

[11] E. Carney, "Artifice and Alexander History," B14 (2000): 263–85; see also D. Ogden in B18 (2007): 75–108.

[12] Quoting (p. 430) M. Brosius (*Gnomon* 78/5, 2006: 426–30), who does not appear to have grasped either the logic or the implications of my discussions in *Darius dans l'ombre*; cf. the more dispassionate review by J.-P. Stronk: http://ccat.sas .upenn.edu/bmcr/2004/2004–03–10.html.

that the search for truth, "the first duty of the historian, tends to be dismissed as a topos, honoured more in the breach than the observance."[13] On the contrary, we cannot assume that all the ancient accounts must of necessity contain "a kernel of historical truth." It is essential to realize that there are veritable historical novels that form part of the Graeco-Roman literature devoted to Alexander,[14] and that the historian has to maneuver constantly along the narrow frontier separating history from romance. The reason for this needs repeating: every ancient book that we make use of is "a literary work in its own right and . . . a product of its own particular context. . . . The work of the historian then becomes an exercise in literary analysis as opposed to traditional source criticism. . . . "[15] Or, to be more precise, the two approaches are not so much opposed to each other as complementary: the Alexander historian must be capable of handling intertextual analysis, along with the many other tools available to him, including, naturally, "traditional source criticism."

Virtually every interpretation should really carry a warning along the lines of, "If we are to believe Diodorus," "If Arrian is not mistaken," "If sources quoted by Plutarch are reliable," "If Curtius's story has some historical basis," etc. Such caveats do not mean that the credibility of the Greek and Latin sources on Darius and Alexander is to be consistently denied. They must, however, be consistently put to the test. These sources can, in fact, be the worst and/or the

---

[13] Despite A. B. Bosworth in the introduction to a somewhat "positivist" article: "Plus ça change . . . Ancient historians and their sources," *Classical Antiquity* 22/2 (2003): 167–98.

[14] See, for example, Briant, *Darius dans l'ombre*: 427–39, 587–88 (on the relations between Alexander and Bagoas).

[15] Quoting M. Flower in B19 (2007): 423.

best tools, depending on the manner in which the historian uses them, and in accordance with the analytical methods used to test them. Moreover, it is easily demonstrable that as long as they are set inside the Achaemenid imperial context—global and/or regional—they can provide information of the first importance. So rather than devoting a special chapter to a discussion of the sources, I have decided to introduce all relevant considerations in context, *i.e.*, when the historian is faced by this or that specific problem of interpretation.

One further point. In spite of the subtle, and sometimes repetitive, studies of the transmission of information and interpretations from one generation of authors to another (generally and conveniently called by the German term *Quellenforschung*), we are more often than not incapable of knowing what the primary sources used in this or that particular instance were. Even when we can name one of the chroniclers of Alexander's time, who are sometimes cited by later users, such information by itself does not help much, as we know virtually nothing of their work, except for a few fragmentary citations, frequently minuscule and often rephrased by authors working with them at second or third hand.

This short book, then, is not intended to rehearse well-established facts so much as to highlight the sometimes profound uncertainties that continue to bedevil our interpretations. My purpose is to introduce students to a world that is harder to understand than it might appear at first sight. Rather than repeat the standard complaints about gaps in the documentation, I should like to suggest that if we set the documents that are available to us each in its appropriate historical context, the history of Alexander may appear less obscure and the methods used to study it less daunting than has been supposed.[16]

Pierre Briant

Kersaint, October 2009

[16] See my remarks and suggestions in "Alexander the Great," in G. Boy-Stones, B. Graziosi, and P. Vasunia, eds., *The Oxford Handbook of Hellenic Studies*, Oxford 2009: 77–85.

Acknowledgments

It is a pleasure to acknowledge here the help and hospitality that I have found at Princeton University Press, ever since my first meeting and discussion with Ian Malcolm at Oxford in November 2007, and then with Rob Tempio at Tampa in April 2008. Since then, all the editorial staff has been very patient and unfailingly helpful. I should also like to acknowledge the help of Salima Larabi, my assistant in the Collège de France, for her help in preparing the index.

Among my colleagues, I would like to thank Claude Rapin (CNRS, Paris), who is one of the top specialists in Central Asian archaeology and historical geography. He very kindly offered to redraw the (highly debated) map of Alexander's campaigns in Bactria and Sogdiana in 329–327, according to his most recent researches and reflections.

Amélie Kuhrt, an outstanding specialist in the Achaemenid and Hellenistic world, has been for decades a real supporter of this book and tried several times to persuade publishers to make it available in English. Given the numerous changes and additions I have introduced to the 2005 French edition, she has considerably updated this translation, which she had originally created for her students at University College London. Throughout the process of translation and editing, she has been a constant help at every stage. We have had many very fruitful discussions and exchanges, including when we were correcting the first set of proofs while drinking some good wine in a nice German *bistrot* at Mannheim. This book and its author owe much to her learning and to her friendship.

Alexander the Great

AND HIS EMPIRE

Introduction

Alexander before the Expedition to Asia Minor (356–334)

Alexander was born in July 356 at Pella, capital of the Macedonian kingdom.[1] His parents were Olympias, daughter of the king of the Molossians, and Philip II, king of Macedon since the death of King Perdiccas in 359. Much has been written about Alexander's psychological heritage, but it is impossible to determine with any certainty which aspects of his character he inherited from his parents, still less which came from one parent rather than the other. His first teacher was Leonidas, a kinsman of Olympias, who had a team of tutors under his direction. When Leonidas's brutal methods did not meet with the expected success, Philip also called in Aristotle, who had opened a school at Mytilene on Lesbos, following his stay with Hermias, tyrant of Atarneus, in Asia Minor. Aristotle instructed Alexander and his friends of the same age for three years (343–340) at Mieza. The extent of Aristotle's influence on Alexander is difficult to assess, but it

[1] On this early period of Alexander's life, see, *e.g.*, B12 (1995): 25–70; B15 (2003): 69–132; B16 (2003): 29–86; B17 (2003): 17–105; B18 (2007): 1–74, 109–124; for a synthesis, see Bosworth, *Conquest and Empire* (1988): 5–23. On all this, apart from the Athenian sources, Arrian represents a relatively reliable narrative (I.1–10), on which see the detailed commentary of Bosworth, *Commentary*, I (1980): 45–96; see also Diodorus XVII.2–3; 5.1–2; 8–15; Plutarch, *Alex.* 1–14 (Hamilton, *Commentary* [1969]): 2–36; Justin XI.1–4 (Yardley-Heckel, *Justin, Books 11–12* [1997]: 72–104).

1

is safe to say that several modern authors tend to overesti-
mate it. Wilcken, writing in 1931, stressed that Aristotle
brought Alexander into close contact with Greek culture.
We should remember, however, that the Macedonian court
had already been welcoming Greek artists for several gen-
erations, and that Alexander himself displayed a strong pas-
sion for the great works of Greek literature, especially the
Iliad. Greek culture was an integral part of his schooling,
and this may reflect Macedonian royal tastes as much as the
specific influence of Aristotle. It is generally assumed that
Alexander remained in contact with Aristotle, at least down
to 327, when he had the philosopher's nephew Callisthenes
condemned to death. But even on this point, the documentation, where it exists, is vague.[2]

Early on Philip associated his son with him in the exercise of power and its related responsibilities. When he left
on campaign against Byzantium in 340, he entrusted the
conduct of the kingdom to the sixteen-year-old Alexander,
taking care to surround him with experienced advisors. The
young prince was also given the opportunity to mount an
expedition against the formidable Thracians and to found a
military colony (Alexandropolis). At the famous Battle of
Chaeronea (338) between Macedonians and Greeks, he
commanded the left (offensive) wing of the cavalry. After
the battle he, together with Antipater, was sent on an embassy to Athens bearing the ashes of the Athenians killed
on the battlefield.

This good relationship between father and son, however, suffered a setback in 337, when Philip repudiated Olym-

[2] See for example the critical reservations of J. S. Romm ("Aristotle's Elephant
and the Myth of Alexander's Scientific Patronage," *AJPh* 110/4 [1989]: 566–75),
which I find more persuasive than the position taken by L. Bodson, "Alexander the
Great and the Scientific Exploration of the Oriental Part of His Empire," *Ancient
Society* 22 (1991): 127–38.

pias and married Cleopatra, a Macedonian princess, and Alexander along with his mother went into exile to Epirus. Thanks to the intervention of Demaratus of Corinth a reconciliation was effected fairly rapidly. A less serious quarrel between father and son erupted when Philip proposed Arrhidaeus, Alexander's half-brother, as groom to the daughter of Pixodaros the dynast of Caria, causing an anxious Alexander to intrigue secretly with the dynast. The affair ended with the banishment of a number of Alexander's best friends, who were thought to have misled him (Nearchus, Harpalus, and Ptolemy, among others).

In October of the year 336, there took place at Aigai a marriage between Cleopatra, daughter of Philip and Olympias (now reconciled), and a Molossian prince named Alexander. On the occasion of this royal wedding, Pausanias, a young Macedonian nobleman, murdered Philip, stabbing him in broad daylight in the middle of the theater where the celebration was taking place. This, at least, is one possible story, but it is a version beset with many uncertainties respecting both the chronology of the events and the background of the various episodes. There has been much debate—both in the past and continuing to the present day: Did Pausanias act on his own, or was he egged on by Olympias, by the Achaemenid court, or even by Alexander? Did Alexander perhaps feel his position to be insecure in the aftermath of the Pixodaros affair, so that he was drawn to join in a plot against his father, or at least not to oppose it? Again the documentation is very scanty, as it depends on Plutarch's story (*Alex.* 10.1–8), on the basis of which it is possible to assume, or not, that Alexander had reason to fear that he might not succeed Philip. It is important to stress once more: there is no text nor any argument that can furnish convincing proofs. We are reduced to either believing Plutarch or not, and/or to deciding

3

whether he was motivated by a concern for historical truth or by his wish to make a splash in literary circles.[3]

As soon as Alexander became king, he proclaimed to the Assembly of the Macedonian people (the representatives of the *ethnos*)[4] his desire to continue his father's work. He must surely have conducted the funerary ceremonies in the royal necropolis of Aigai, as doing so would publicly and definitively confer dynastic legitimacy upon himself as the new king.[5] He immediately made preparations to ensure calm and stability within the Greek communities. Philip's death and the new king's youth had given rise to hopes among Alexander's enemies: ambitious members of the Macedonian nobility, the barbarians on the frontiers of the kingdom, the Greeks, and, of course, at the Achaemenid court. Alexander set about methodically disabusing them. He began by ordering a bloody purge of the Macedonian nobility: Philip's murderer Pausanias was executed, as were a number of real and suspected pretenders, while some nobles chose to

[3] M. Hatzopoulos ("A Reconsideration of the Pixodaros Affair," in *Studies in the History of Art* 10, Symposium Series I, Washington DC [1986]: 59–66) comments: "The Pixodaros affair, if not simply invented, was completely different from what Plutarch's account would have us believe. . . ." (p. 62). Against this, V. French and P. Dixon ("The Pixodarus Affair: Another View," *AncWorld* 13 [1986]: 73–86) support Plutarch, whose "high regard for the truth, and his desire to avoid malice" they stress (p. 85).

[4] This is not the place to review at length the historiography of this issue. Since my discussion in *Antigone* (1973): 237–350 (based on Aymard's earlier studies), innumerable articles rejecting my suggestions have appeared (most recently the one by E. M. Anson in *Classical Philology* 103 [2008]: 135–49). On this "new orthodoxy," see the critical analysis and interpretations of M. Hatzopoulos, *Macedonian Institutions under the Kings* I, Athens 1996: 37–42 (historiography) and 261–322 ("The Common Assembly").

[5] Since Manolis Andronikos's first discoveries at the site in 1977, there have been endless debates about the identification of the tomb as that of the dead king. The bibliography is too enormous to be cited here: see the information collected and presented by Elizabeth Carney at http://people.clemson.edu/~elizab/aegae.htm and http://people.clemson.edu/~elizab/Tombbib.htm#Tombbib.

flee to Asia and offer their services to the Great King. Alexander "descended" on Greece, silenced his opponents (particularly those in Athens), and was granted the title of commander of the war against Persia, thus renewing the Corinthian pact of 338. The third stage in his consolidation of power was a campaign along the Danube and in the Balkans (spring 335) that resulted in the Thracians offering their submission. Alexander clearly wanted to be sure of the situation to his rear. He broke off his Illyrian campaign and within thirteen days had advanced upon the Greeks who, misled by news of his death, were preparing to rebel. When Thebes refused to surrender, Alexander took it by storm and left the fate of the captured city in the hands of the Greeks gathered at Corinth: Thebes was razed to the ground, a powerful warning to the other Greek cities. Alexander displayed more clemency towards Athens, which had given Thebes clandestine support. Of the orators, only Charidemos was exiled and sought refuge at the Great King's court. Everything was now ready. Philip's death had delayed the start of the great expedition into Asia by no more than a few months.

Chapter I

The Major Stages of the Conquest (334–323)

From Granicus to the Fall of Tyre
(May 334–Summer 332)

During the first two years of the war, Alexander twice faced the Persians in a set battle: first, on the banks of the Granicus (May 334), and then at Issus in Cilicia (November 333). Both were victories for the Macedonians, but neither was decisive, and the Persians were twice able to mount dangerous counterattacks on the West Anatolian littoral and in the interior of Asia Minor. At this stage, Alexander while at Miletus decided to dismiss his fleet (summer 334) and threw himself into the effort of conquering the coasts. His progress was held up for months, from January to the summer of 332, by the resistance of Phoenician Tyre. But that summer marked a turning point for the expedition. For the first time Alexander's rearward lines were secure. The Macedonian fleet was reconstituted in 333 and effectively took the initiative against the Achaemenid squadrons. Throughout this period, Darius continued actively to prepare his troops in Babylonia.[1]

This chapter is no more than a narrative and chronological introduction, in a very stripped down form. In my discussion of each of the major stages, I am indebted on the one hand to Arrian's chapters, which remain fundamental to all reconstructions of events, and, on the other, to current historical commentaries on Arrian (Bosworth), Quintus-Curtius (Atkinson), Justin (Yardley-Heckel), and Plutarch (Hamilton).

[1] See Arrian I.11.3–8, 12–29, II.1–24: Bosworth, *Commentary* I (1980); 96–257; Atkinson, *Commentary on Q. Curtius* I (1980): 77–324; Yardley-Heckel, *Justin*

The landing took place in spring 334, with the Persians apparently making no attempt to use their maritime superiority. The satraps of Asia Minor drew up their army on the bank of the Granicus, where they were defeated and driven off the field by Alexander (May 334). This victory allowed him to march southward through Asia Minor, liberating the Greek cities, punishing any who resisted and removing tyrants allied to the Persians. Sardis, the center of Achaemenid control, surrendered readily. By contrast, Halicarnassus, which had been fortified by Orontobates and further strengthened by Memnon, mounted a fierce resistance to Alexander, forcing him to abandon, for a time, his efforts to take the city (end of summer 334). At Miletus (summer 334) Alexander sent his fleet home, having decided that his best strategy against the superior Achaemenid fleet would be to attack its bases and sources of supply. After leaving Halicarnassus in autumn 334, he embarked on a tough winter campaign (334/333), and despite the resistance of several cities, including Aspendos, he was able to seize the Lycian and Pamphylian coast. He then advanced via Pisidia and Greater Phrygia towards central Asia Minor, and while awaiting the final surrender of the garrison, installed Antigonus Monophthalmos at the satrapal capital Kelainai. Alexander spent several months at Gordion (spring 333), where he received reinforcements from Greece and Macedon. Meanwhile Memnon, who had been ordered by Darius to reconquer the coast, mounted an extremely dangerous counterattack along the Asia Minor coast, but he died in the summer of 333 (July–August) outside the walls of Mytilene on Lesbos.

In about May or June of 333, Alexander proceeded to-

11–12 (1997): 104–150; Hamilton, *Plutarch. Commentary* (1969): 36–64. On Alexander's campaign in Asia Minor, see also P. Debord, *L'Asie Mineure au IVe siècle*, Paris-Bordeaux 1999: 427–92.

wards Cilicia, only touching western Cappadocia, which he turned into a satrapy (though in name only), and breached the Cilician Gates, which the Persians had left inadequately defended. He captured Tarsus, the capital of Cilicia, and established there the first imperial mint striking coins in his own name. While King Agis of Sparta was trying to link up with the Persian admirals, Darius deployed an immense army, but the eventual confrontation at Issus was unsuccessful for the Persians (November 333). This victory gave Alexander hostages in the persons of the mother, wife, daughters, and a son of the Great King, who were captured at Damascus after the battle. It also improved his finances through the seizure of the treasuries in Damascus;[2] but above all, it enabled him to march against Phoenicia, which he needed to control in order to deprive the Persians of their maritime forces. Most of the Phoenician cities—Arados, Byblos, Tripolis, and Sidon—for a variety of reasons, offered no resistance and "were allowed to retain" their traditional institutions. By contrast, Tyre put up a lengthy resistance to the Macedonian siege, during which time the Persian armies tried to mount a counterattack to Alexander's rear in Asia Minor.

At the beginning of spring 332, Alexander won a major victory when the Phoenician and Cypriot contingents left the Persian fleet and joined his side. Tyre fell a few weeks later. At this point, the plan Alexander had formulated at Miletus—namely, to gain the upper hand on the naval front—had proved more or less successful.

[2] For the inventory of the treasure taken by Parmenion, see Athenaeus XIII.608a and Briant, *History*: 293–94. *Contra* E. F. Bloedow ("'Back to Damascus.' The Story behind Parmenion's Mission to Seize Dareius' Field Treasure and Baggage Train in 333 BC," *Prudentia* 29 [1997]): 131–42, I do not think that we have to see here a desire on Alexander's part to relegate Parmenion to a position of secondary importance. Parmenion had, in fact, been put in charge of leading the expedition in Syria (Q. Curtius IV.1.4).

From Tyre to the Euphrates
(Summer 332–Summer 331)

In the course of the following year, the two adversaries continued their preparations for the battle that each hoped would be decisive. Alexander seized Egypt, retraced his steps to Tyre, and from there marched towards the Euphrates and Tigris. Meanwhile, Darius gathered his forces. And all the while Agis of Sparta went on with his preparations to move against Macedon.[3]

Alexander was now sure of the forces to his rear and so continued his conquest of the Phoenician coast; only Gaza resisted vigorously until November 332. Now, accompanied by his fleet under the command of Hephaestion, he arrived in Egypt, where its satrap Mazakes, known from his coinage (Fig. 2), was without his military forces and surrendered the satrapy to Alexander.

The Macedonian fleet simultaneously continued the reconquest of the islands and cities that had been occupied by the Persians in 333 (including Chios and Lesbos). In November 332, the Macedonian admiral Hegelochos was able to make a positive report to Alexander and hand over the pro-Persian tyrants, of whom those from Chios were deported to Elephantine Island.

Alexander knew very well how to show his respect for Egypt's gods and temples, and his stay in Egypt from the end of 332 to the spring of 331 was marked by two important events: his journey to the Siwa Oasis, where he consulted the oracle of

---

[3] See Arrian II.25–27, III.1–5; Bosworth, *Commentary* I (1980): 257–85; Atkinson, *Commentary on Q. Curtius* I (1980): 324–74; Yardley-Heckel, *Justin 11–12* (1997): 150–57; Hamilton, *Plutarch. Commentary* (1969): 64–78.

Fig. 2. Reverse of a silver coin struck in the name of Mazakes, satrap of Egypt, c. 333/332 BC. Imitation of the Athenian owl type. The satrap's name, in Aramaic, is at the right. Cabinet des Médailles (Paris), Inv. 1973.1.190, all rights reserved.

Amun, and the foundation of Alexandria (the first city of that name), which was destined to become a center of major importance under Alexander's successors, the Ptolemies.

Alexander left Egypt in the spring of 331, after reorganizing its administration. He retraced his route as far as Tyre, along the way putting down a revolt in Samaria that is mentioned by Quintus Curtius (IV.8.9–10):

[Alexander received] news of the death of Andromachus, whom he had placed in charge of Syria; the Samaritans had burnt him alive. To avenge his murder, he hastened to the spot with all possible speed, and on his arrival those who had committed this heinous crime were delivered to him.

This is all we know of the revolt, but it shows at the very least that this region continued to be restless after Issus.[4] After entrusting the province to another governor, Alexander moved towards the Euphrates via Damascus and Aleppo. One source of anxiety continued during this period, namely the situation in Europe, where Agis III of Sparta was a growing threat.

The End of Darius and the Final Submission of Greece
(Summer 331–Summer 330)

Alexander's aim now was to defeat Darius and take him captive. He succeeded in his first aim at Gaugamela on October 1, 331,[5] but failed to capture Darius. Opposition in Persis (Fars) and Darius's attempt to turn the situation round prevented Alexander from mounting an immediate attack on the Iranian Plateau. When Alexander was free to leave western Iran after the burning of Persepolis (May 330), Darius was abandoned by his chief commanders, who assassinated him and left his corpse in a Parthian village (July 330).[6]

[4] There is also some inferential evidence on the Samaria revolt; see the appendix. For the administrative arrangements, see Bosworth, "Government of Syria," CQ 24/1 (1974): 46–51.

[5] The exact date is given by a Babylonian tablet, which dates the battle to the 24th day of the month Ululu of Darius's year 5: Van der Spek, *AchHist* XIII (2003): 297–99; Kuhrt, *Persian Empire* I (2007): 447–48.

[6] See Arrian III.6–22: Bosworth, *Commentary* I (1980): 285–348; Atkinson, *Commentary on Q. Curtius* I (1980): 374–479; Yardley-Heckel, *Justin 11–12* (1997): 157–80; Hamilton, *Plutarch. Commentary* (1969): 90–116.

While Alexander was in Egypt, Darius gathered rein-forcements. He deployed an immense army east of the Tigris at the site of Gaugamela. The battle (October 1, 331) re-mained undecided for a considerable time, but was eventu-ally won by the Macedonians. Darius abandoned the field and, following a meeting in Arbela, reached Ecbatana in Media, where he hoped to raise fresh troops. Meanwhile Al-exander moved towards the great royal residences of the em-pire: Babylon, Susa, Persepolis, and Pasargadae.

The European situation continued very worrying. Agis III was again engaged in open warfare, but was defeated by Antipater at Megalopolis in October of 331, at about the time of Alexander's victory at Gaugamela.[7] In response, Al-exander increased the favors extended to the Greek cities in order to persuade them to remain loyal. But anxieties about the situation in Europe were not a major factor in Alexan-der's plans, and they do not explain his decision to burn the palace of Persepolis in the spring of 330.

Alexander's advance enabled him to take control of the major Achaemenid residences. Babylon offered no resis-tance despite its military strength; in fact the Achaemenid commanders and the Babylonian community leaders came out of the city to welcome the conqueror. They accepted Alexander's authority, and in a text of the period he is even accorded the archaizing title "King of the World." In Baby-lon, Alexander took a decision of major significance, namely the appointment of an Iranian satrap. He was also able to appropriate the huge Achaemenid treasuries in Babylon and Susa. The march to Persepolis was more hazardous. Alexander had to fight against the Uxians, a tribe of herds-

---

[7] Given the gaps in the documentation, the precise chronology of Agis's war, as it relates to Alexander's progress across Achaemenid teritory, remains debated.

men who controlled a pass on the route between Fahliyun and the Persian Gates and then do battle against the Persian troops who were occupying the Gates. He reached Persepolis in mid-January, and for several months he was undecided as to his course of action; eventually he decided to destroy the city, which was the symbol of Achaemenid domination.

In spring 330 Alexander began his pursuit of Darius, who had decided to withdraw eastward. As Alexander was now sure of his control in Europe, he disbanded the Greek contingents of the League of Corinth, which had not really played any significant part during the conquest. This put an end, once and for all, to the fiction that the campaign was a "Hellenic war." The decision was taken at Ecbatana in Media, as he was about to follow Darius onto the Iranian Plateau. Meanwhile, a plot was formed against Darius, and his chief commanders abandoned him. Bessos and Nabarzanes arrested the Great King, held him prisoner, and then murdered him in the summer of 330. Although his advance had been very rapid, Alexander had thus failed to take Darius alive. Henceforth he cast himself in the role of the Great King's avenger.

Guerillas in the Eastern Satrapies and Macedonian Opposition (Summer 330–Spring 327)

The next phase was one of the most difficult, perhaps the most difficult, of the entire expedition. Before marching on India, which he had already planned to conquer, Alexander had to overcome resistance in the eastern satrapies: mainly in Areia, Drangiana, Sogdiana, and Bactria. At the same time he had to deal with Mace-

donian opposition emanating both from the ranks of the army and from its commanders.[8]

Initially, Alexander tried to reach Bactria, where Bessos had proclaimed himself king, adopting the name Artaxerxes. The army took the old route, known later as the Khorassan Road, via Parthia and Areia. But he was called back by the re-volt of Satibarzanes in Areia, who was supported by Bessos. Alexander had to subjugate the satrapy anew; he then decided to approach Bactria from the south, conquering Drangiana, Arachosia, and the Parapamisadae. This offensive undermined Bessos's plans: he abandoned Bactria before being surrendered to Alexander.[9] From then until 327, the Sogdian chief Spit-amenes and a number of petty local princes led the resistance.

Alexander now increasingly adopted features of Ach-aemenid kingship, received Persian nobles into his entou-rage, and began to behave more and more like an absolute ruler, behavior that provoked fierce opposition among the Macedonian nobility. The chief episodes in the story of the struggle between the king and his inner circle are the trial of Philotas and the execution of Parmenion, the murder of Kleitos and the *proskynesis* affair.

For their part, rank and file Macedonian soldiers were by now openly disgruntled. The savagery of the guerilla war had demoralized them, and they wanted to go home.

[8] See Arrian III.23–30, IV.1–22; Bosworth, *Commentary* I (1980): 348–79, II (1995): 13–141; Atkinson, *Commentary on Q. Curtius* I (1994): 164–260 [ends at VII.2.38]; Yardley-Heckel, *Justin 11–12* (1997): 198–235; Hamilton, *Plutarch. Commentary* (1969): 116–61.

[9] There continues to be much uncertainty and debate about these campaigns; see A. B. Bosworth, "A Missing Year in the History of Alexander the Great," *JHS* 101 (1981): 17–37, and G. Grenet and C. Rapin, "Alexander, Aï Khanum, Ter-mez: Remarks on the Spring Campaign of 328," *Bulletin of the Asia Institute* 12 (1998): 78–89. On the recently published Aramaic documents from Bactria and the information to be gathered from them, see the appendix.

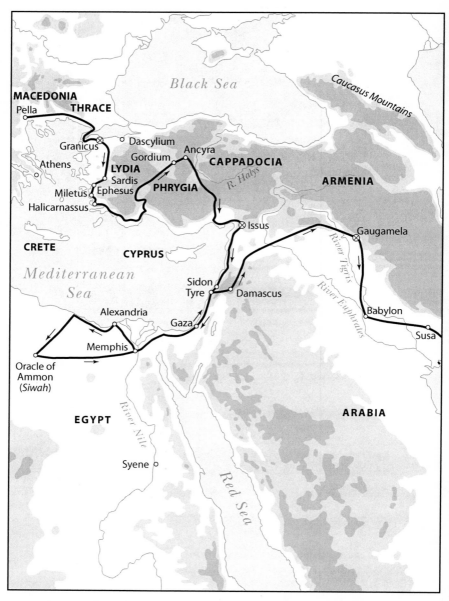

Map 1. Alexander's conquest: the main routes and battles. For a close up of the area in the gray box, see map 2.

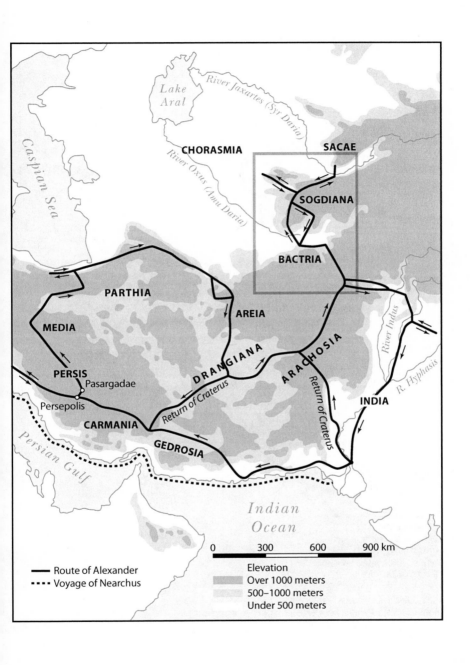

Lake Aral

River Jaxartes (Syr Daria)

River Oxus (Amu Daria)

Caspian Sea

CHORASMIA

SACAE

SOGDIANA

BACTRIA

PARTHIA

MEDIA

AREIA

DRANGIANA

ARACHOSIA

River Indus

PERSIS

Pasargadae

Return of Craterus

R. Hyphasis

Persepolis

CARMANIA

Return of Craterus

INDIA

Persian Gulf

GEDROSIA

Indian Ocean

0   300   600   900 km

——— Route of Alexander

- - - - Voyage of Nearchus

Elevation
Over 1000 meters
500–1000 meters
Under 500 meters

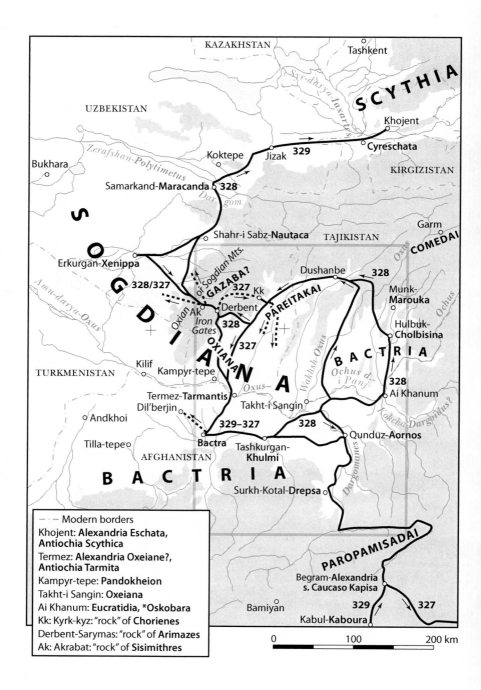

KAZAKHSTAN

Tashkent

SCYTHIA

UZBEKISTAN

Khojent

S-darya Jaxartes

Koktepe
Jizak **329**
Cyreschata

Bukhara

KIRGIZISTAN

Zerafshan-Polytimetus

Samarkand-**Maracanda** **328**

Dargom

S
O
G
D
I
A
N
A

Garm

Shahr-i Sabz-**Nautaca**
TAJIKISTAN

COMEDAI

Oxus

Erkurgan-**Xenippa**

Dushanbe
328

Munk-
Marouka

Amu-darya-Oxus

328/327

of Sogdian Mts.

GAZABA?
327 Kk

Ochus

Hulbuk-
Cholbisina

Oxian Ak
Iron
Gates
Derbent
328

327

PAREITAKAI

B A C T R I A

Wakhsh-Oxus

Kilif

TURKMENISTAN

Kampyr-tepe

O
X
I
A
N
A

Ochus d.
i Panj

328
Ai Khanum

Oxus

Termez-**Tarmantis**
Dil'berjin

Takht-i Sangin

Kokcha-Dargoidus?

Andkhoi

329–327
328

Qunduz-**Aornos**

Tilla-tepe

Bactra
Tashkurgan-
Khulmi

Dargomanes

AFGHANISTAN

B A C T R I A

Surkh-Kotal-**Drepsa**

-·- Modern borders

Khojent: **Alexandria Eschata,**
Antiochia Scythica

Termez: **Alexandria Oxeiane?,**
Antiochia Tarmita

Kampyr-tepe: **Pandokheion**

Takht-i Sangin: **Oxeiana**

Ai Khanum: **Eucratidia, *Oskobara**

Kk: Kyrk-kyz: "rock" of **Chorienes**

Derbent-Sarymas: "rock" of **Arimazes**

Ak: Akrabat: "rock" of **Sisimithres**

PAROPAMISADAI

Begram-Alexandria
s. Caucaso Kapisa

329
327

Bamiyan

Kabul-**Kaboura**

0   100   200 km

Maps 2 and 3. Alexander's 329–27 campaigns in Bactria and Sogdiana. Map 3 (above) provides a closer view of the boxed area in map 2 (left). Copyright Claude Rapin and the French Archaeological Mission in Uzbekistan (MAFOUZ), 2009.

At the same time, Alexander embarked on a series of measures that would have important long-term consequences. He founded a number of cities and military colonies to control principal strategic points and to keep watch over the peoples in the satrapies and along the frontiers,[10] but the policy aroused the opposition of Greek colonists in Bactria. Alexander also initiated a policy of collaboration with the Iranian aristocracy, a growing number of whom were appointed as satraps. Then, in 327, he married Roxane, the daughter of a Bactrian nobleman.

The Conquest of India and the Return via the Persian Gulf (327–325)

Once the eastern satrapies had been conquered, Alexander was able to embark at last on the conquest of India. Following a difficult march, the Macedonians reached the Indus in the spring of 326. In July the army won a victory over Poros on the banks of the Hydaspes, which seemed to open vast horizons to Alexander. He, however, set the limit to his conquests on the banks of the Hyphasis river (summer 326), and then sailed down the Indus. Afterwards he returned to Persis and Elam, moving along the coast of the Persian Gulf.[11]

[10] A German-Uzbek team has brought to light a fortress that the archaeologists date to 328; it would have been founded by Alexander in the course of his Sogdiana campaign; see L. M. Sverchkov, "The Kurganzol Fortress (on the History of Central Asia in the Hellenistic Era)," *Ancient Civilizations from Scythia and Siberia* 14 (2008): 123–91.

[11] See Arrian IV.1.23–30, V–VI.1–28; Bosworth, *Commentary* II (1995): 141–360 (ends with the mutiny on the Hyphasis), Arrian V.29; Yardley-Heckel, *Justin 11–12* (1997): 235–68; Hamilton, *Plutarch. Commentary* (1969): 161–87.

During the summer of 327, Alexander left Bactria and headed for Alexandria-in-the-Caucasus, a location of prime strategic importance controlling the principal routes. Part of the army he entrusted to Hephaestion and Perdiccas, with orders that they gain control of the right bank of the Cophen (Kabul River) and prepare for the arrival of the rest of the army on the Indus. Alexander threw himself into the conquest of the region traversed by the tributaries of the left bank of the Cophen. In the spring of 326, after a difficult march, he reached the Indus and joined up with Perdiccas and Hephaestion, who had reached the river some time before.

Several Indian princes submitted to Alexander, including Omphis and Taxiles, to whom Alexander granted their kingdoms. Taxiles informed him of the danger presented by another Indian ruler, Poros. The battle against this formidable foe was fought on the River Hydaspes in July of 326. It was probably the toughest battle fought in Asia by the Macedonians, who were terrified by the charging elephants of Poros's army. Alexander's "elephant coinage," whose date of issue is disputed, commemorated the heroic deeds of the Greeks and Macedonians on the Indian campaign (Fig. 3).

Alexander's troops were now suffering battle fatigue. Anxious to return to Macedon and frightened by rumors of the potential dangers of an expedition beyond the Hyphasis, they mutinied and demanded that the king stop the war of conquest. Alexander was forced to move on to the next stage of his plans: namely, sailing down the Indus and returning via the Persian Gulf. This campaign resulted in the often brutal subjugation of several Indian peoples and gained Alexander control of the main routes linking India and the Persian Gulf.

Fig. 3. Reverse of the silver coin known as the "Poros decadrachm," illustrating combat between Indians (on an elephant) and a horseman (Alexander?). Cabinet des Médailles (Paris), Inv. 1978–21. Photo: copyright O. Bopearachchi. Drawing from A. B. Bosworth (B15 [2003] 164, fig. 4).

The Last Years (324–323)

During the two final years following Alexander's return from India, his actions went far beyond the bounds of his original aims:[12]

- He persisted in plans to gain control of the Persian Gulf, mounting three expeditions as a prelude to the conquest of the Arabian coast. The construction of a fleet and a harbor in Babylon formed parts of the same project;
- He took over the administration of the hydraulic system in Babylonia and Elam;
- He subjugated those peoples who still refused to acknowledge him as king (the expedition against the Cossaeans in 323);
- He capped his policy of collaborating with Darius's lieutenants by concluding marriages at Susa (324), and through the formation of a Macedonian-Iranian army (324/323).

[12] See Arrian VI.28–30, VII; Yardley-Heckel, *Justin 11–12* (1997): 269–99; Hamilton, *Plutarch. Commentary* (1969): 187–217.

- It is possible but by no means certain that he contemplated a campaign to the West.

When Alexander died in Babylon on the night between the 10th and 11th of June, 323,[13] he had conquered the entire Achaemenid empire, as it had been formed by Cyrus, Cambyses, Darius I, and their successors. Despite the precarious nature of Macedonian control in certain regions, this was a huge achievement. But how did Alexander manage to overcome the various forms of opposition that he faced in the course of his military progress? What were his aims, and how long had he been planning the enterprise? What was the nature of the resistance organized by Darius, and how extensive was it? These are the questions we shall now consider.

[13] The date of his death is mentioned in passing on a Babylonian tablet ("The king is dead"); see *e.g.*, R. J. Van der Spek, in *Orientalia* 69/4 (2000): 435.

Chapter II

The Origins and Objectives of the Conquest

No sooner do we broach the question of Alexander's projects and aims than we enter a territory that is very poorly sign-posted. The ancient sources outdo each other in the superlatives extolling Alexander's ambition and the enthusiasm for conquest with which he treads in the footsteps of his "divine ancestors." But not a single writer considers the question that most exercises the modern historian: What exactly was Alexander's objective? We read, for example: "In early spring Alexander marched to the Hellespont. . . ."[1] or "Alexander assembled his military commanders and his noblest Friends and put forward for discussion the plan for crossing to Asia. When should the campaign start and how should they conduct the war?"[2] But the writers seem either to have known nothing about the plans for the impending campaign, or else to have considered the question of insufficient interest to merit discussion. It is therefore only by cautiously and painstakingly following in Alexander's footsteps that the historian may hope to discern evidence of the nature, the scope, and the limits of his territorial goals.[3]

---

[1] Arrian I.11.3.
[2] Diodorus XVII.16.1.
[3] See my *Lettre ouverte à Alexandre le Grand*, Arles 2008: 67–108.

The Unsatisfactory Nature of Explanations Based on Personality and Psychology

Among the explanations for Alexander's campaign put forward by several ancient authors and, in their wake, by some modern historians, are those that place emphasis on Alexander's psychological makeup, and in particular on irrational elements that may have occupied a place in his psyche. Some suggest that Alexander's extraordinary and exalted character was due in large part to his psychological heritage from Olympias, a devotée of the Dionysiac cult who indulged "her sensibilities to the full and without restraint" (G. Radet). Others think that at certain points in his life Alexander was motivated by his desire to imitate, or even to identify himself with, Homeric heroes and gods or demigods, such as Dionysos and Herakles. Finally, quite a number of writers (V. Ehrenberg among them) see Alexander allowing himself frequently to be led by *pothos*. This psychological concept, very hard to define precisely, is understood by these writers as an irrational and irresistible desire to excel, to go ever further in exploring the world and oneself.[4] Such interpretations present us with an "irrational" Alexander, who cannot be understood by means of rational or, better, political analysis. They belong to a certain type of historiography that is well illustrated by Georges Radet, in whose view, "the rules of normal psychology" are "inapplicable to a hero who feels the blood of Herakles and Achilles coursing through his veins."[5]

[4] V. Ehrenberg's interesting observations on Alexander's *pothos* (1933) are reprinted in B2 (1966): 74–83.

[5] *Alexandre le Grand*, Paris 1931: 17. (The idea goes back to the eighteenth century; it appears in the article "Alexandre" of the *Encyclopédie* [*Supplément* I, 1776].) On Radet's book, see E. Borza's remarks in U. Wilcken, *Alexander the Great*, New York 1967: xviii.

Such recreations of Alexander have by no means disappeared from historiography, even to this day. They reflect their advocates' surprising confidence in the depictions of Alexander that we find in the ancient sources. Yet there can be no doubt that their authors did not hesitate to knowingly embroider reality in order to exalt the superhuman character of the king and his enterprise.

Alexander was certainly brought up to admire the heroes of whom Homer sang, and he was undoubtedly moved by the emotional impulses and hopes that young men, whose lullabies spoke of Achilles' exploits and fate under the walls of Troy, were bound to nurse in their breasts. He was very much a man of his time in the way he interacted with the heroic past as constructed and reconstructed by Homer and his commentators, as well as with myths and stories of the gods. We are unlikely to be far wrong if we impute to him a love of glory, a wish to construct his historical persona in terms that would survive him, as well as a desire to identify himself with mythical and divine conquerors, such as Herakles and Dionysos. Alexander was certainly also moved by a deep desire (*pothos*) to encounter for himself distant countries, rivers, and seas. But to reduce his expedition to a personal adventure runs the risk of landing us in a position of some absurdity. This *pothos* or ambition need not be understood as linked exclusively to the irrational. Here, for example, is an illustrative passage from Arrian:

> On reaching Pasargadae and Persepolis, Alexander was seized with a desire (*pothos*) to sail the Euphrates and Tigris into the Persian sea and to see the outlets of these rivers into the sea, as he had seen the outlets of the Indus. (VII.11)

We should note that by the time of this voyage (early in 324), Susa and Elam had been under Macedonian occupation for nearly seven years. So the *pothos* in this instance is quite distinct from the conquest as such. At this point, Alexander wanted to reconnoiter his territorial, riverine, and maritime domains, and *personally* to take possession of them.

The risks Alexander took in the course of the expedition were calculated ones: he never embarked on a new phase without being certain of the situation to his rear or without informing himself about the country he was trying to conquer.[6] He led thousands of men into regions often poorly known (to Greeks and Macedonians) and hostile and would hardly have risked losing his army purely for the sake of glory or in order to obey some irrational impulse.[7]

Obviously the task of enquiring into Alexander's ambitions and great deeds is important, but following the ancient writers in devoting page upon page to it leads to the assumption that the only obstacles Alexander had to overcome were his own strategic and psychological weaknesses. Such an assumption obscures collective motivations for the war. Even an individual as outstanding as Alexander belongs to a historical context, with which he has to engage.[8] One of the major problems of Alexander's history is, in fact, precisely the tension from 330 onwards between the collective wish of the Macedonians and the ever more personal quality with which Alexander sought to invest his rule.

---

[6] On this occasionally contested issue (E. Badian, in I. Worthington, ed., *Ventures into Greek History* [1994]: 285–89), see E. Borza in his *Makedonika* (1995): 223–24, and D. Engels, "Alexander's Communication System," CQ 30/2 (1980): 327–40.

[7] This point, too, remains hotly debated; see, for example, E. Badian in *Gnomon* 1975/4: 48–57; Bosworth, *Alexander and the East:* 165–85; and D. Engels, *Alexander the Great and the Logistics of the Macedonian Army*, Berkeley, CA 1978: 110: "Every detail of the expedition [in Gedrosia] was planned in advance."

[8] See M. Austin's highly relevant observations, "Alexander and the Macedonian Invasion of Asia: Aspects of the Historiography of War and Empire in Antiquity," 1993, in B17 (2003): 118–26.

A preoccupation with Alexander's character has yet another disastrous consequence, namely that of making the Persian enemy disappear from the scene, as though Alexander was quite alone, engaged in a personal adventure. Recent work on Achaemenid history and the greater attention that is today paid to the global picture makes it essential to bring Darius III and his circle back into focus, as well as the empire for which they fought so bitterly, using resources and skills that were far from negligible.

The Heritage of Philip II

In W. W. Tarn's well-known formulation, "the primary reason why Alexander invaded Persia was, no doubt, that he never thought of *not* doing it: it was his inheritance."[9] The English historian wanted to indicate with these words that the idea of the conquest originated largely with Philip II. Polybius expressed exactly the same sentiment in a famous passage dealing with the Hannibalic Wars (III 6, 8–14), by referring to Philip's war against the Persians. He sought to establish the differences between the underlying reasons, the pretext, and the beginnings of the war against Persia.[10] While the beginnings properly speaking (*arkhē*) might date to Alexander's reign (he writes), Philip II had long before made considerable preparations, on a diplomatic as well as a military level. After his victory over the Greeks at Chaeronea (September 338), he convened at Corinth a meeting of

---

[9] *Alexander the Great* I, Cambridge 1948: 8 (italics Tarn).
[10] On Polybius's image of Alexander, see R. Billows, "Polybius and Alexander Historiography," in B14 (2000): 286–306.

the delegates of the Greek cities and states. The result of the meeting was the formation of the League of Corinth.

The League's functioning and its member states are known to us only very partially. The major institution was the communal council (*synedrion*), made up of the delegates. Macedon as a state was not a party to this—only the Macedonian king, in a purely personal capacity. The League's charter forbade any change of constitution, war between member states, and any attack on Philip's kingship or that of his successors. These measures served to create stable relations between the cities of a kind that Greece had never known, despite attempts to achieve them in the classical period.[11]

Philip's intention was obviously to ensure a situation of lasting calm in Greece. From this point on, he turned his attention to planning the Asiatic war. After Chaeronea, "Philip spread the word that he wanted to make war on the Persians on the Greeks' behalf and to punish them for the profanation of the temples."[12] That is why, in 338, he had the *synedrion* of the League vote for a "war of reprisal," with the direction of military operations ceded to him under the title *strategos autokrator* ("general with full powers"). After 338, the pretext for the war (to use Polybius's distinction) was clearly established: officially, Philip was only acting on a mandate granted him by the Greeks united by the *Pax Macedonica*. As for the material means needed, these would be ready to hand as every member state of the military alliance was required to send a contingent.

---

[11] On the League, see the concise presentation by M. Farraguna, "Alexander and the Greeks," B15 (2003): 98–107; further, E. Poddighe in B20 (2009) chapter 6, "Alexander and the Greeks: The Corinthian League," 99–120.

[12] Diodorus XVI.89.1.

But Philip did more than just create a pretext for the war. We can date its very beginning to his reign when, in 336, he landed an advance force of 10,000 men in Asia, under the command of his trusted friends Parmenion and Attalus. Despite undeniable reverses inflicted by Memnon in 335, Parmenion was able to hold Abydos, the ideal place for landing an army crossing from Europe. Alexander was thus engaged in the war well before 334.[13]

Unfortunately, it is hard to be precise about Philip's territorial objectives.[14] According to the tradition that reports negotiations between Alexander and Darius, Philip's old companion Parmenion disagreed with Alexander and urged him to give a favorable response to diplomatic overtures from Darius, who proposed ceding Asia west of the Euphrates to Alexander. According to Georges Radet, "this dialogue draws a marked contrast between Philip's programme of circumscribed ambitions and Alexander's doctrine of unlimited conquest." But quite apart from the fact that this interpretation is completely speculative, it is based on texts whose factual reliability is highly questionable. It also perpetuates the stereotype that pits the "reasonable objectives" of the father against the "unquenchable ambition" of the son. This reflects the rhetoric of a literary genre well known since antiquity.[15]

Many suggest that Philip's project was inspired directly by the writings of Isocrates. This Athenian orator was a rep-

[13] See E. Badian, "Alexander and the Greeks of Asia," *Studies Ehrenberg* 1966: 39–43, reprinted in B22 (2010).

[14] E. F. Bloedow's article ("Why Did Philip and Alexander Launch a War against the Persian Empire?" *L'Antiquité Classique* 72 [2003]: 261–74) is somewhat disappointing; the same is true of M. Brosius's analysis ("Why Persia Became the Enemy of Macedon," *AchHist* XIII [2003]: 227–37).

[15] See E. A. Fredricksmeyer, "On the Final Aims of Philip II," (1982), reprinted in B17 (2003): 54–64.

resentative and apostle of Panhellenism and, after realizing the impossibility of the Greek cities ever uniting, he pinned his hopes on Philip. But we should not draw hasty conclusions about the extent of Isocrates' influence; Philip was perfectly capable of assessing for himself the realities of the situation in Greece (which he had himself done much to create) and of defining his policy on that basis. Isocrates was certainly not the person who gave Philip (or Alexander) the idea of making war on Persia, nor that of creating a league founded on the notion of a "Common Peace." Further, the goals of Isocrates and Philip were ultimately irreconcilable: while Isocrates hoped to use Macedonian power to launch Athens onto the path of renewed imperialism, Philip was determined to use the League of Corinth for his own ends. There is then no basis for asserting that Philip adopted Isocrates' program, which envisaged the settlement by Greeks of Asia Minor "from Cilicia to Sinope."[16]

From this point on, it is plain that Macedonian concerns overtook Isocrates' dreams. Philip embarked on the enterprise with two aims in view: he would direct the expedition both as general of the Hellenes, in order to avenge Greece—hence the invention (or rather reinvention) of the useful formula of a "war of reprisal"—and as king of the Macedonians, in order (officially, at least) to punish the Persian attacks on Perinthus and Thrace. To these, Alexander added a third motive: taking revenge for the murder of Philip, which Macedonian propaganda attributed to Achaemenid court intrigue.[17]

---

[16] Isocrates, *Philippus* para. 146. On this issue, see M. Flower's nice analysis, "Alexander the Great and Panhellenism," in B14 (2000): 96–135, esp. pp. 97–107 (*Panhellenism as a Popular Ideology*).

[17] Arrian II.14.5: "My father was murdered by conspirators whom you Persians organized. . . ."

Alexander and the Royal Territories
of the Achaemenids

The ancient authors report that, on debarking, Alexander made a gesture that was considered highly significant:

> On reaching the mainland, Alexander first hurled his spear into the soil as into hostile territory. (Justin XI. 5, 10)

> There he flung his spear from the ship and then leapt ashore himself the first of the Macedonians, signifying that he received Asia from the gods as a spear-won prize (*chora doriktetos*). (Diodorus XVII.17.2)

Because the texts aim to impress on the reader Alexander's heroism, these accounts are not by themselves sufficient to allow us to evaluate the extent of his territorial ambitions. But the appointment of Macedonian satraps and administrators in the conquered provinces immediately following the victory on the Granicus leaves us in little doubt. Thus, at Daskyleion, capital of Hellespontine Phrygia, whose satrap Arsites had committed suicide in the wake of the defeat:

> Alexander . . . made Kalas satrap of the territory Arsites ruled, ordering the inhabitants to pay the same tributes (*phoroi*) as they used to pay to Darius; natives who came down from the hills and gave themselves up were told to return home. . . . He also sent Parmenion to take over Daskyleion, and this he duly did, the guards having evacuated the place. (Arrian I.17.1–2)

Everywhere in Asia Minor we can see the same policy being applied, symbolized by the reimposition of the tribute of the barbarians, *i.e.* the tribute paid to Darius. At the very least such attitudes and decisions imply that, well before landing, Alexander's goals went far beyond those of Isocrates. Despite arguments that have often been put forward, it is difficult to accept that Alexander's main objective could have been a "war of reprisal," intended to be limited in time and space.

"War of Liberation" and "War of Reprisal": The Limits of Alexander's Philhellenism

In accordance with the decision of the *synedrion* and the *hegemon*, contingents were levied in the cities and states of the League. These formed a not insubstantial part of Alexander's army: 7,000 infantry (out of a total of 32,000) and 2,400 horse, if one includes the Thessalian cavalry (out of a total of 5,500). But with the exception of the Thessalian cavalry, these contingents played a somewhat marginal role during the expedition. As for the Greek fleet, the king dismissed it in summer 334 at Miletus.

The participation of these contingents in Alexander's campaign served two purposes. First, their presence underscored the Panhellenic character of this "war of reprisal," led by the "general of the Hellenes." In the course of the campaign, Alexander did not fail to take measures designed to drive this idea home. After the victory on the Granicus (334), for example:

> he sent to Athens 300 Persian panoplies to be set up to Athena in the acropolis; he ordered this inscription to be attached: "Alexander, son of Philip, and the Greeks, except the Lacedaemonians, set up these spoils from the barbarians dwelling in Asia." (Arrian, I.16.7)

But we need to place that gesture in context. The Macedonians were not forgotten. The families of the Macedonian cavalrymen who had fallen in battle also received gifts, namely a remission of personal and property taxes.[18] Further, Alexander ordered Lysippos to make sculptures of the twenty-five Companions (*hetairoi*) who fell in the course of the battle; they were set up at Dion.[19]

Moreover, a rapid analysis shows very clearly that Alexander's Hellenic fervor grew and waned in direct proportion to the military and strategic difficulties he encountered in the course of the war. His goodwill gestures increased markedly at precisely the moment when Agis III of Sparta threatened Macedonian control in Europe. Thus, in spring 331, he agreed to release the Athenian mercenaries who had been taken at the Granicus, whereas earlier at Gordion (spring 333) he had brutally turned down the Athenian request that he do so. At that point, when the Persian reconquests at sea put the success of the expedition in serious danger, Alexander had decided that this was not the moment "to lessen the terror with which he had inspired the Greeks."[20] After the victory at Gaugamela (October 331), which Alexander likened to the Greek victories over the Persians at Salamis (480) and Plataea (479), "he wrote (to the Greeks) that all tyrannies had been abolished and they could govern themselves in accordance with their own laws."[21] At Susa (December 331), before he had received the news of Agis's defeat, he returned to Athens the statues of the tyrant slayers, which Xerxes had taken in 480.[22]

---

[18] Arrian I.16.7 (*ateleia*); see Bosworth, *Commentary* I (1980): 125–26.

[19] Arrian I.16.4. The statues were later taken to Rome on the occasion of Q. Metellus Macedonicus's triumph in 146 BC; cf. G. Calcani, *Cavalieri di bronzo*, Rome 1989.

[20] Arrian I.29.5–6.

[21] Plutarch, *Alex.* 34.2.

[22] Arrian III.16.8, who adds that the statues could still be seen at the Kerameikos in his day.

Finally, modern authors have not failed to point out that the levy of Greek contingents also served to ensure tranquility among the Greek states, an important concern for Alexander. In other words, the allied troops were little more than hostages. It is significant that the only open revolt in Greece during this period emanated from Sparta which, of course, had refused to join the League, and the war against Sparta is the last occasion on which we see the *synedrion* of Corinth in action.

The liberation of the Greek cities in Asia Minor is presented by many ancient authors as one of Alexander's main objectives. In the cities governed by oligarchs or tyrants his arrival was definitely regarded as a deliverance. In Ephesos, for example, the re-establishment of democracy unleashed a chain of communal violence, and Alexander was forced to intervene to put a halt to the massacre of the tyrant's partisans.[23] But alongside such enthusiastic receptions, there were several instances of resistance and revolt, as, for example, in the small cities of southern Asia Minor, which Alexander had to take by force in the course of a tough winter campaign (334/333).

Alexander's policy toward the Greek cities during his conquest of Asia Minor was dictated to a large extent by their attitude toward him. In other words, he felt himself entitled to use the Greek laws of war in dealing with rebels, and thus to deal as a sovereign with cities and their inhabitants.[24] Freedom was not inherent to the Greek city as W. W. Tarn thought—rather it was a boon granted by Alexander, and therefore precarious. The best illustration of this comes from the Pamphylian city of Aspendos. Alexander

[23] Arrian I.17.10–12.
[24] Cf. the discussion by Farraguna in B15 (2003): 109–15, with references to the epigraphic sources.

originally granted it freedom from a garrison and halved its tribute in silver (50 talents) and materials (horses). The Aspendians were thus guaranteed autonomy, but when Alexander learned that the city was refusing to keep its side of the agreement, he turned back and *imposed* a new settlement, which transformed Aspendos from an autonomous into a subject city.

> He demanded their most influential men as hostages, the horses they had previously promised and a hundred talents in place of fifty; they were to be subject to the satrap appointed by him and to pay a yearly tribute to Macedon and an adjudication was to be held about the territory they were accused of having annexed by violence from their neighbours. (Arrian I.27.4)

It is tempting to ask the question that Sealey posed in relation to the foundation of the Delian League by Athens in 478/7: Did the Greek cities of Asia really wish to be "liberated"?[25] The yielding of Athens, Thebes, and Sparta to Achaemenid ultimatums in the fourth century must have made the cities of Asia mistrustful of the enthusiasm of their European sisters. Had they not accepted the King's Peace in 386, which endorsed Persian domination on the Anatolian coast? Further, Alexander's brutal treatment of Thebes in 335 cannot but have raised dire fears about how the Macedonian ruler envisaged his relationship with the Greek cities. There is also, finally, the consideration that during more than two centuries of "cohabitation," a certain *modus vivendi* had been established between the Greeks of Asia and the Achaemenid administration.

[25] "The Origin of the Delian League," in *Studies V. Ehrenberg*, Oxford (1966): 233–55.

The Conquest of India and Return via the Persian Gulf

Historians have hypothesized a strikingly wide range of motives for Alexander's campaigns in India and the Persian Gulf. Explanations currently in vogue are, first, the attraction that the unknown had for Alexander; second, his desire to identify with Herakles and Dionysos; then, his unquenchable desire (*pothos*); and, finally, his taste for geographical exploration and his commercial ambitions. The problem is to know which of these was the decisive motivation. We should also ask where precisely Alexander wanted to lead his troops and from what point on he had nursed the idea of conquering India.

In the first place, it is wrong to see Alexander as a kind of Christopher Columbus. Although his expedition did effectively provide the Greeks with new information about geography and plant and animal species in the conquered countries, it must be stressed emphatically that the king did not discover any virgin territory. Darius I had conquered the Punjab and the Indus Valley, and had integrated them into the Achaemenid empire, of which they still formed (at least nominally) a part.[26] Alexander did not venture into the unknown; in fact, he received information from the Indian princes who rallied to his side, and later from local guides.[27] Alexander's main aim must certainly have been to conquer for himself the whole of Darius I's empire and gain control of the political assets and fiscal resources of the region as the Great Kings had done.

Everything suggests that Alexander's territorial ambitions

[26] See Briant, *History*: 754–57 and the bibliography on pp. 1027–28; also E. Badian, "The King's Indians," in B7 (1998): 205–24.

[27] On Alexander's informants, see Bosworth, *Alexander and the East*: 66–97.

were very real and that, in 334, he had an idea that was broadly clear but vague in detail on the extent of the world he was planning to conquer. It is more than likely that the reason for his clear-sightedness was that this world had already been conquered by the Achaemenids. Did Alexander, after the defeat of Poros, intend to go beyond the Achaemenid boundaries to the Ganges and the "outer ocean," as certain ancient texts assert? Or was his sole aim to sail down the Indus and return via the Persian Gulf?[28] Given the many serious problems, it seems doubtful that it was only the soldiers' "mutiny" on the Hyphasis that forced Alexander to turn back.[29] The evidence suggests, rather, that the descent of the Indus and the return along the Persian coast of the Gulf was part and parcel of a long-term plan: Alexander intended to follow the boundaries of the Achaemenid empire and take control of it in its totality, and the Indus was, of course, the empire's eastern frontier.

The Problem of the "Last Plans"

When it comes to Alexander's territorial plans we confront a paradox: the only explicit discussion of the topic is also the one that rouses the greatest skepticism. Several authors assert that in 323 Alexander entertained plans to conquer the western Mediterranean basin. According to Diodorus (XVII.4.1–6), papers outlining his projects (*hypomnemata*)

---

[28] For Alexander's knowledge of the Ganges plain, see Bosworth, *Alexander and the East*: 186–200, "Alexander and the Ganges: A Question of Probability."

[29] See F. Holt's convincing analysis, "The Hyphasis 'Mutiny': A Source Study," *Ancient World* 5 (1982): 33–59; also, Bosworth, *Commentary* II (1995): 337–60 ("The Mutiny at the Hyphasis"); and W. Heckel, "Alexander the Great and the Limits of the 'Civilized World,'" in B16 (2003): 147–74.

were discovered after the king's death; Perdiccas, an important figure in the succession, presented these to the soldiers (who rejected them):

> It was proposed to build a thousand warships, larger than triremes, in Phoenicia, Syria, Cilicia and Cyprus for the campaign against the Carthaginians and the others who live along the coast of Libya and Iberia and the adjoining coastal region as far as Sicily; to make a road along the coast of Libya as far as the Pillars of Heracles (Straits of Gibraltar) and, as needed by so great an expedition, to construct ports and shipyards at suitable places; to erect six lavish temples, each at a cost of fifteen hundred talents; and, finally, to establish cities and to transplant populations from Asia to Europe and in the opposite direction from Europe to Asia, in order to bring the largest continents to a common unity (*homonoia*) and to friendly kinship by means of intermarriages and family ties. . . . A tomb for his father Philip was to be constructed to match the greatest of the pyramids of Egypt, buildings which some count among the seven greatest works of man. When these memoranda had been read, the Macedonians, although they applauded the name of Alexander, nevertheless saw that the projects were extravagant and impracticable and decided to carry out none of those that have been mentioned.

There can be few texts that have excited so many divergent comments, because the problems raised by the tradition are extremely complex.[30] Although Arrian says that he is convinced

---

[30] Two articles on this topic, by Hampl (1953) and Schachermeyr (1954), are reprinted in B2 (1966): 307–44. More recently, see above all E. Badian's discussion, "A King's Notebooks" (1967), reprinted in B22 (2010); Badian thinks it perfectly consistent with Alexander's character that he may have toyed with such plans, but he concludes: "What Alexander's plans were is . . . equally irrecoverable" (p. 204).

of Alexander's insatiable ambition, he nevertheless declares himself incapable of taking a position on this: "I for my part have no means of conjecturing with any accuracy, nor do I care to guess." (VII.1.4) In some respects, the modern historian finds himself in the same impasse.

The coherence of the plans attributed to Alexander is probably fictitious. It is based in large part on a link made between a proposed expedition to circumnavigate Arabia as far as Egypt and a project to take the war into the western Mediterranean. The projected circumnavigation was certainly ventured, but both the squadrons operating from the Persian Gulf as well as those setting out from the Red Sea met with insurmountable obstacles. This is not surprising given the unprecedented technical problems of such an undertaking. We cannot assert that Alexander simply followed Achaemenid traditions here, because, despite Darius I's claims (on one of the stelae he set up along the canal he had reopened between the Nile and the Red Sea, c. 500–490), there was never a direct *regular* line of communication between the Red Sea and the Persian Gulf during the period of Persian rule. In any case the Persians lost control of the Red Sea when Egypt gained independence around 400.[31] In 324/323, Alexander's chief interest was rather to lay his hands on the Arabian coast of the Persian Gulf,[32] as Nearchus and he had done on the Persian coast. If we allow him only the smallest modicum of a military commander's foresight, then

---

[31] See most recently, J. F. Salles, "Travelling to India without Alexander's Logbooks," in H. P. Ray and D. T. Potts, eds, *Memory as History: The Legacy of Alexander in Asia*, New Delhi 2007: 157–69, with bibliography. Salles retains his earlier doubts (excessive in my view) about the reality of the sea voyage from India to Egypt, which an Achaemenid fleet achieved in Darius I's reign (the voyage of Scylax, known to Herodotus [IV.44]).

[32] Arrian VII.19.2.

we must admit that he can have had no intention of risking his forces on a fool's enterprise. These observations do not, of course, totally undermine the possibility that Alexander had western plans, but the sources available to us are insufficiently reliable to justify that conclusion.

Chapter III

Resistance to the Conquest

Neither Alexander's steadfast advance nor his ultimate success should mislead one into thinking that his campaign proceeded smoothly, with no setbacks. On the contrary, he had to cope with prolonged resistance from Darius and the Achaemenid forces (334–330). The danger was increased by the very real possibility that a revolt in European Greece might coincide with the Persian counterattacks (333–331). During the three years following Darius's death (330–327), the Macedonian army faced the threat of defeat in Bactria and Sogdiana. At the same time, opposition developed among the Macedonian nobility, as well as growing reluctance among rank and file soldiers.[1]

The Resistance of Darius (334–330)

The Forces Available

It would be a great mistake to underestimate either the capacity of the Achaemenid empire for resistance or the abilities of its leader Darius. In 334, the balance of numbers favored the

---

[1] See my *History* (2002): 817–71, 1042–51, and W. Heckel's chapter "Resistance to Alexander the Great," in L. Tritle, ed., *The Greek World in the Fourth Century*, London and New York 1996: 189–227 (the focus here is exclusively on military matters).

Persians. Against Alexander's Macedonian force of 25,000 infantry and around 2,000 cavalry—to which must be added the Greek and mercenary contingents (3,000 allied cavalry and approximately 7,000 infantry soldiers) the Achaemenid empire was able to mobilize several armies and naval forces of unquestionable strength (though we need to be wary of the numbers reported by the sources).[2] The Great King's financial resources were also virtually limitless, since he had the accumulated treasures of Susa, Ecbatana, Persepolis, and Babylon at his disposal, as well as the provincial treasuries (for example in Sardis and Tarsus), and the many mints in the western satrapies.

Contrary to a commonly held idea, the Achaemenid empire had not fallen into a state of accelerated decline in the fourth century. Nor is there any sign of an economic crisis or of widespread discontent. The Great King was always able to rely on the loyalty of the great Persian families and on the cooperation of local elites. This does not mean, however, that the empire was in a state of total tranquility. There had been revolts, including a recent one in Egypt (the so-called revolt of Khababash[3]), but overall imperial authority was accepted inasmuch as the unity of the empire rested on the recognition of its regional and local diversity.[4]

What is true is that the Macedonian army under Alexander's command was decidedly superior to the Persian forces in technique and maneuverability. Alexander had inherited

[2] On Alexander's army at the start of his campaign, see Bosworth, *Conquest and Empire*: 259–66, and B. Strauss in B15 (2003): 142–47; on the Achaemenid armies and the way they are depicted in the classical sources, see Briant, *History*: 587–99, 793–800, 979–80, 1034–38.

[3] For this incident, see Briant, *History*: 1017–18; and more recently, S. Burstein, "Prelude to Alexander the Great: The Reign of Khababash," *AHB* 14 (2000): 149–54.

[4] For the situation in the Achaemenid empire, see Briant, *History*: 693–813, 1006–41, and my two chapters on Darius's empire in B19 (2009).

from Philip an army fully trained in fighting set battles, and he was himself an unrivalled tactician with an exceptional ability to adapt to new situations. When facing Darius's royal forces, which were only mobilized in exceptional circumstances, the Macedonians responded as a quasi-professional army. But the Achaemenid armies also included some highly trained contingents, and Darius had introduced technical innovations.[5] He further enjoyed naval superiority, which in 334 gave him potential control of the Aegean.[6]

Alexander's Strategic Vulnerability

To explain how things turned out, it is not enough to compare numbers of combatants and fighting methods. At the strategic level, it should be stressed that in May 334 Alexander's position was not as firm as it might appear. Although, contrary to the impression given by our sources, he had sufficient financial reserves,[7] he could not afford to make a single mistake. He knew very well that any setback would encourage the "revanchists" in the Greek cities. In effect, Alexander was condemned to win.

As important as his victory was (Alexander was not, after all, pushed back to the sea), the Battle of the Granicus did not guarantee that Alexander would be able to subjugate Asia Minor without meeting any opposition. A substantial part of the Persian forces had managed to flee the battlefield, and had retreated to Miletus, where Memnon took command, and then to Halicarnassus after the fall of

[5] See Briant, "The Achaemenid Empire," in K. Raaflaub and N. Rosenstein, eds., *Soldiers, Society and War in the Ancient and Medieval Worlds*, Cambridge, MA 1999: 105–28.
[6] See Arrian's analysis, I.18.3–9, 19–20.1.
[7] See Le Rider, *Alexander the Great:* 73–84.

Miletus. The determination of these troops to resist was strong, particularly among the Greek mercenaries, whose willingness to abandon Darius was undermined by Alexander's unmitigated brutality in the aftermath of battle.[8]

Memnon and Orontobates withstood the siege of Halicarnassus, and Memnon was commissioned by Darius to reconquer the islands and the coast.[9] The situation for Alexander, who was held up by the defenders of Halicarnassus (summer 334), was serious because he had committed himself to fighting with his back to the sea. At Miletus (July–August), he had decided to dismiss his fleet, which was made up of Greek contingents. According to Arrian (I.20.1), he was convinced that they stood no chance of defeating the numerically and qualitatively superior Phoenician fleet. Moreover, Alexander lacked the funds necessary to maintain this naval force and feared a revolt by the Greek crews. He decided to fight Persian maritime superiority on land, by bringing under his control all the regions from which Darius raised his fleet and crews—the coasts of Lycia, Pamphylia, Cilicia, and Syro-Phoenicia.[10]

Nothing suggests that this strategy was a "colossal error."[11] On the contrary, it seems to have given Alexander the advantage. But, as with all major strategic shifts, there was the risk, as Alexander was surely well aware, of being caught on the horns of a dilemma: on the one hand there was Darius, who was engaged in a mass mobilization, and on the other there was Memnon, whose considerable success in

[8] Arrian I.16.2–3 (Bosworth, *Commentary* I: 124–25).

[9] See Arrian I.20.2–10, 21–23.

[10] See in particular Arrian I.19.8: "[The Persians], from want of water and other things, were as good as besieged in their ships"; and I.20.1: "he was to overcome the ships from dry land."

[11] The quotation comes from Bosworth, *Commentary* I: 141–43.

his attempt to reconquer the Anatolian coast raised hopes (ultimately illusory) among the Greek cities of Europe.[12] Ancient authors attach an exaggerated importance to the role played by Memnon. In fact his death at Mytilene on Lesbos (summer 333) did not immediately change the situation. Pharnabazus and Autophradates, who succeeded Memnon, did not slacken their efforts, but led a major offensive, taking many islands where the terms of Persian control, as laid down by Artaxerxes II in 386, were reaffirmed.[13]

When Alexander left Gordion in Phrygia (about July of 333), his situation was not very secure. Shortly before the battle at Issus, his enemies were dangerously close to effecting a juncture with Agis of Sparta, who was preparing to join Autophradates and Pharnabazus on Siphnos when news of the battle arrived.[14] The victory at Issus allowed Alexander to proceed down to the Phoenician cities—Tyre first and foremost—which was at this point his main goal. He never thought of going in pursuit of Darius. Contrary to a convention that accuses him of "excessive rashness" (surprisingly it still has its adherents), it was not in the Macedonian king's interest to launch a pursuit of Darius, for that would have seen him arriving in Babylonia completely unprepared. That would have been madness, as Arrian (II.17) makes clear in a speech he puts in Alexander's mouth.

Thousands of Persian horsemen, led by prominent commanders, fled north after the defeat at Issus. They retreated in good order along the royal road and established them-

[12] See in particular Arrian II.1–2. According to Worthington (ZPE 147 [2004]: 59–71), Alexander had concluded a treaty with Athens in the summer of 333 to fight the Persians on the seas.

[13] Cf. Arrian II.1.3–4, 2.2. On the naval operations of Memnon and his successors, see Bosworth, Commentary I: 177–84 and Briant, History: 823–28; on the figure of Memnon in Greek sources, Briant, History: 790–91, 820–23, 1035, 1043.

[14] Arrian II.13.4–6.

selves in the regions that remained, *de facto*, outside Macedonian control, namely Cappadocia and Paphlagonia. There they conscripted fresh troops, soon gathering substantial forces under their command (end 333–beginning 332). Coins minted at Sinope in the names of Mithropastes, Orontobates, and Hydarnes should certainly be linked to this Persian enterprise, the intent of which was to reconquer the whole of Asia Minor between the Halys and the sea.[15]

At the same time, Darius began to assemble a new army in Babylonia and the Phoenician fleet continued to control the sea. In Europe, Agis of Sparta, though isolated, was making preparations. Meanwhile Alexander was held up for several months at Tyre, where the inhabitants were prepared to resist as long as possible in order to allow the Great King to complete his preparations: "They thought also that they would receive great gifts (*megalai doreai*) from the king for such a favour."[16] Alexander, for his part, could not raise the siege without forfeiting his chance of conquering the Phoenician coast, on which the future success of his campaign depended. Everything hung in the balance, and he risked being caught in a pincer movement.

In this exceptional situation, he entrusted the command of all his troops in Asia Minor to Antigonus the One-Eyed, satrap of Greater Phrygia. Antigonus was an outstanding warrior, who succeeded, with the help of the other satraps (Kalas, Nearchus, and Balakros), in crushing the Persian counterattack in the spring of 332. Alexander must have been greatly relieved by these victories, which coincided with the arrival of substantial naval reinforcements that completely changed the balance of forces:

[15] Texts, interpretation, and bibliography in Briant, *History:* 823–30, 1043–44; and Kuhrt, *Persian Empire*, I (2007): 441–42.

[16] Diodorus XVII.40.2.

Meanwhile, Gerostratus king of Aradus and Enylus of Byblus, learning that Alexander held their cities, left Autophradates and his fleet and arrived with their own contingents, and with the Sidonian triremes, so that a total force joined him of some eighty Phoenician sail. There arrived also at the same time triremes from Rhodes, nine, in addition to their state-guardship, three from Soli and Lycia, and a fifty-oar from Macedonia, its captain Proteus, son of Andronicus. Soon also the kings of Cyprus put in at Sidon with about 120 sail, having learnt of Darius's defeat at Issus, and scared by Alexander's hold over all Phoenicia. (Arrian II.20.1–3)

The fall of Tyre in the summer of 332 made it possible for Alexander to achieve the objective he had set himself in the previous summer of taking the Achaemenid navy's land bases. But the game was not yet played out. Though shocked by the news of Issus and much weakened, Pharnabazus continued his activities until autumn 332; Alexander encountered difficulties in taking the stronghold of Gaza, fiercely defended by its governor Batis; and all the while Darius was assembling and equipping his new army.

Darius and the Persians versus Alexander

Must we, then, blame the Achaemenid defeat on the inferiority of the Persian command? Many modern historians put most of the blame on Darius's shoulders, describing him as a coward on the battlefield and an incompetent diplomat. This was already the image propagated by the Greek sources which, filled with an overweening superiority complex, automatically applied certain standard words when speaking of the Persians: weakness, luxury, sensuality, drunkenness, cowardice. Historians of today, as a majority of recent studies suggest, tend to regard Darius as not quite the incompe-

Fig. 4. Portrait of Darius. Detail of the Alexander Mosaic, ca. 100 BC, Naples National Archaeological Museum. Drawing from Niccolini, "Musaico scoperto in Pompei il di 24 ottobre 1831," *Real Museo Borbonico* 8, Naples 1832, Pl. XL.

tent strategist of former historical opinion.[17] Nor was he the "feeble king" regularly presented by the ancient writers.[18]

It is somewhat puzzling that Darius did not use his immense naval superiority to block access across the Hellespont, and that he did not rush to place himself at the head of his army in order to push Alexander back to the sea. His inaction seems even more inexplicable when we consider

[17] For recent research on Darius, see the bibliography.
[18] On the motif of "Darius's flight," see in particular Briant, *Darius dans l'ombre:* 335–46, 525–55.

that he cannot have been ignorant of Alexander's preparations. The main point to acknowledge is that, in the absence of full documentation, the curious absence of the fleet remains unexplained, or, at least, that none of the explanations usually put forward are more than hypotheses.[19] As for the tardy mobilization of the royal army, it is as well to emphasize that throughout Achaemenid history general mobilizations were rare. It is likely that in 334 Darius and his advisers regarded the Macedonian landing as yet another attempt that was destined to fail. Was this a fatal mistake? Facile *post eventum* reasoning certainly suggests that it was, but the Persians in 334 could not have foreseen the future. When the Macedonians landed, history was still waiting to be written.

And so it was that Darius followed standard practice in his response to Alexander.[20] He ordered Arsites, satrap of Hellespontine Phrygia, to take command of the forces supplied by the various satraps of Asia Minor and to confront the Macedonian army in a set battle in Phrygia. Ancient authors describe a war council held by Arsites. According to Arrian and Diodorus, two contrasting tactics were proposed. As usual, Diodorus gives a prominent place to Memnon, who apparently advocated a scorched earth strategy. Arrian writes:

> Arsites, however, is reported to have said in the Persian Council that he would not suffer one house belonging to his subjects to be burned: the Persians supported Arsites, having suspicions of Memnon, thinking that he was delaying warlike operations for the sake of the office he held from the king. (I.12.10)

[19] On this still-unresolved point, see Briant, *History:* 818–20, 1043.
[20] Briant, *History:* 822–23.

In taking Memnon's side, Diodorus asserts that Arsites and the Persian leaders rejected his suggestion, "since his advice seemed to be beneath the Persians' dignity (*megalopsychia*)" (XVII.18.3). On the basis of Diodorus's statement, a myth has come into being that the Persians, blinded by their "chivalrous nature," adopted a plan that Diodorus could easily classify as disastrous. In fact, however, the war council was not in a position to pick and choose its tactics. Arsites and his colleagues had received the order from Darius: they were to face Alexander in a set battle. Given the superior manpower of the Persians as well as the assumed superiority of their cavalry, Arsites may well have believed that he had a good chance of emerging the victor.

Darius's supposed panic in the face of the first Macedonian successes is mainly deduced from an ancient tradition relating to his "territorial concessions."[21] The Alexander biographers report that, after Issus, Darius thrice (or twice) made diplomatic overtures in an attempt to recover his family, which had been taken prisoner after the battle. That he may have done so is undeniable. But the accounts add that when Alexander was at Tyre (332), and then again when he was crossing the Euphrates (summer 331), the Great King promised him the hand of one of his daughters, and that he offered to cede him part of the imperial territory, either up to the Halys (332), or as far as the Euphrates (331). Quintus Curtius adds that the territory to be ceded was the dowry of a princess offered to the Macedonian king.

But the sources are confusing and contradictory. Diodorus's source asserted that, during a council with his advisers, Alexander produced a forged letter from Darius (XVII.39.2).

[21] On the following, see Briant, *History*, 823–28, 1044–45 (annotated bibliography); on the literary motifs, Briant, *Darius dans l'ombre*: 323–29, 582–83 (recent bibliography).

It is indeed very likely that Darius initiated negotiations with Alexander after Issus and that letters and embassies passed between the two camps. It is further very likely, as we have noted, that the Great King tried to obtain the return of those members of his family who were being held as prisoners-of-war in the Macedonian camp, and we may well believe that he was prepared to pay a fairly high price to that end. But the suggestion that he was prepared to relinquish any of his territory, first the district between the Halys and the sea, and later the regions west of the Euphrates, is a very different matter. Offers of this kind (at various dates and subject to varying conditions) fit neither his tactics nor the military actions undertaken between Issus and Gaugamela. To the very end, Darius remained determined to fight. This was true even after Gaugamela, when his army was ever more inclined to go over to the side of his adversary.

Although we are not likely ever to learn what the two kings said to one another, it is clear that Darius never dreamed of relinquishing first a quarter and then a half of his empire. He abandoned the battlefield at Issus, together with his family and household, fully aware of what was at stake, namely the survival of the empire. For Darius and his councilors the fate of the Persian empire took priority over the fate of his relatives.[22]

Underground Resistance and Open Revolt in Greece

All the while, Greece did not remain quiescent. When Alexander reached Asia Minor in May 334, he was well aware of the potential dangers. He had confided the task of keep-

---

[22] On this last point, which is absolutely crucial and decisive, see in particular my discussion, *Darius dans l'ombre*: 525–55.

ing watch over the Greek cities to Antipater, leaving him for the purpose an army of 15,000 infantry and 1,500 cavalry.[23] Open revolt began in Sparta, which had refused to join the League of Corinth and had, therefore, not sent a contingent to serve with Alexander. Agis III, who had acceded in 338, thus had his hands free to muster a Spartan army. His aim was to collaborate with the Great King. In 333 he decided to join the Persian side and went to meet the admirals Autophradates and Pharnabazus on the island of Siphnos. Unfortunately for him, his arrival coincided with the news of Darius's defeat at Issus, which destroyed any lingering hopes of leading an orchestrated action against Alexander in both Asia Minor and Greece.[24]

In 331, a revolt broke out in Thrace, where Alexander's general, Memnon, seems to have decided to make a bid for independence. We cannot be sure whether this uprising was deliberately coordinated with that of Agis, but it is clear that Agis began hostilities at the same time. Antipater, fully occupied on the Thracian front, sent his general Korragos to the Peloponnese, where he was defeated and killed. Reading Aeschines (*Against Ctesiphon*, 165), one can imagine the impact of that first defeat of a Macedonian army:

> The Lacedaemonians and the mercenary troops won the battle and annihilated Korragos' army. The Eleans joined them, as well as all the Achaeans except Megalopolis. This city was besieged, and each day we awaited the news of its fall. Alexander had reached the pole and virtually the ends of the earth. Antipater slowly gathered his army and the future was uncertain.

[23] On Antipater and Agis's revolt, see E. Badian, "Agis III: Revisions and Reflections," in I. Worthington, ed., *Ventures in Greek History*, Oxford 1994: 258–92. (I do not share Badian's conclusions.)

[24] Arrian II.13.4–5.

The language is rhetorical yet cautious. But there can be little doubt that Alexander must have anxiously followed the events in the Peloponnese, and he soon took action to challenge Agis. At Tyre in the spring of 331, he finally agreed to release the Athenian mercenaries captured at the Granicus in order to keep Athens on his side and encourage her not to intervene. Shortly afterwards, the admiral Amphoteros was sent "to help those Peloponnesians who had confidence in the outcome of the Persian War, and who were not in the Lacedaemonian camp."[25] Finally, just before setting out for the Euphrates, he ordered Antipater to come to terms (temporarily) with Memnon and to concentrate on Agis. Antipater enrolled contingents from the League of Corinth, and the battle was fought at an uncertain date (autumn or winter of 331?) beneath the walls of Megalopolis. The Spartans were defeated and Agis lost his life. Alexander was still not completely free of his worries, which is why we see him multiplying goodwill gestures towards the European Greeks for several more months.[26]

Agis's revolt certainly aroused in Alexander intense anxiety about the dependability of his European base, but its importance should not be exaggerated. It did not contribute to the decision he took at Persepolis in May of 330.

Resistance and Reprisals in the Eastern Satrapies (330–327)

Far more serious was the fierce resistance of the eastern satrapies after Darius's death. Almost three years were needed

[25] Arrian III.6.3.
[26] See for example, Arrian III.16.7–8 (at Susa in November–December 330).

just to subjugate Bactria and Sogdiana, under the command of Bessos and then Spitamenes.

Bessos's Failure and Spitamenes' Guerilla War

After playing a principal role in the conspiracy against Darius, Bessos returned to his satrapy of Bactria. He persuaded the population to rise up "in order to defend their freedom," and proclaimed himself king, taking the name Artaxerxes. He could rely on support from Satibarzanes, satrap of Areia, whom Alexander had retained in his post. The new Artaxerxes was joined in Bactria by Oxyartes and Spitamenes, together with a strong Sogdian contingent, which reinforced the 7,000 horsemen raised by Bessos.

Bessos's plan was to devastate the Bactrian plateau as Alexander advanced through it and then to give battle to a Macedonian army that would be on its knees as a result of the privations it had suffered. But Alexander launched an offensive in the spring of 329 that took the Bactrian leaders by surprise and caused them to withdraw beyond the Oxus, burning the boats they had used for the crossing. The 7,000-strong Bactrian cavalry eventually abandoned them. The Macedonian army managed to cross the Oxus on skins stuffed with straw. Oxyartes and Spitamenes betrayed Bessos and surrendered him to Alexander.[27]

The capture of Bessos did not solve Alexander's problems. Spitamenes now took the lead in a far more dangerous revolt. Unlike Bessos, who cleaved to rigid Achaemenid military strategies (i.e., set battles), the Sogdian chieftain knew exactly how to deploy against Alexander the natural and human resources of Sogdiana and Bactria, lands that bristled with natural strongholds. He also knew that the Macedonian

[27] Arrian III.25.3, 28.8–9, 29.6–7, 30.1–5.

army was not adept at avoiding ambushes or detecting deception. A multitude of towns and garrisons offered resistance and forced Alexander to embark on an exhausting course of siege warfare. The situation here was very different from that in the west, where the fall of the satrapal capital generally meant the surrender of the satrapy as a whole.

Spitamenes adopted the tactics of relentless harassment and trickery against the Macedonian army, which was now forced to capture and secure innumerable strongholds throughout the countryside. As soon as the Macedonians appeared their opponents would vanish, only to reappear suddenly in some unexpected spot. Faced with such an unpredictable adversary, Alexander tried to improve his army's mobility, detaching contingents and sending them off in pursuit of Spitamenes, whenever and wherever he appeared. The Sogdian leader, moreover, had enlisted Scythians, who had been greatly troubled by Alexander's northward move and the foundation of Alexandria-on-the-Jaxartes (329). In spite of all, the Macedonian soldiers gradually adapted to guerilla warfare, and Alexander was soon in a position to levy cavalry from Bactrian and Sogdian nobles who allied themselves with him.

The help given by the Scythians turned out to be slight and equivocal, however, as Arrian (IV.17.4–5) makes clear:

> These Scythians are in great poverty, and also, since they have no cities and no settled habitations, so that they have no fear for their home, they are easily persuaded to join in this or that war.

Arrian's stereotypical image of the nomad notwithstanding,[28] we should note that not all the people of the steppes

[28] Cf. Briant, *État et pasteurs:* 9–56.

took up arms against Alexander. Thus, the resistance of the Sacae beyond the Syr Darya (Jaxartes) was brief, and a peace was soon concluded (329). When the Sogdian and Bactrian contingents defected to Alexander's side, the Massagetae killed Spitamenes, with the idea that this "would persuade Alexander not to pursue them." When we add to this the fact that the Bactrian and Sogdian nobility submitted in increasing numbers, then the "national" character generally attributed to this revolt must be questioned.[29] Rather than a single revolt, it is better to talk of a series of revolts, of varying levels of strength and duration, and with differing objectives.

An event that occurred in the winter of 329/8 illustrates well the harsh nature of the fighting and the real dangers encountered by Alexander's forces. Alexander had himself taken part in the capture of the city of Cyropolis, and he was just setting out to cross the Jaxartes, when Spitamenes succeeded in retaking Samarkand and its citadel.[30] The king sent against him as swiftly as possible an army made up, according to Arrian, of 1,500 mercenary infantry soldiers and 1,400 cavalry, of whom six hundred were the renowned Companions. The engagement or, more likely, ambush took place in the valley of the Zeravshan (Polytimetus) River, where the light and highly mobile horsemen of the steppes crushed the Macedonian army operating under what seem to have been less than able commanders. Arrian describes the disaster as follows:

> In this confusion and disorder the Scythians charged down
> in large numbers, so that of cavalry no more than forty escaped, and of foot-soldiers about three-hundred. (IV.6.2)

[29] Cf. Briant, *L'Asie centrale*: 77–88.

[30] See in particular Arrian IV.3.6–7, 6.1–2; Quintus Curtius VII.6.24, 7.30–38; cf. Bosworth, *Commentary* II: 22–25, 32–37; N. Hammond (1991) in B11 (1994, III): 109–15.

In order to understand better the danger encountered by the Macedonians in 329–327, we should also remember that the king and his commanders had to fight on several fronts. In order to face Bessos as swiftly as possible, Alexander had to leave barely subjugated regions in the hands of Iranian satraps whose loyalty was as yet untried. Bessos was even in a position to appoint a satrap in Parthia. In Areia, Satibarzanes rebelled twice, and two other Iranian governors, Arsakes in Areia and Oxyartes in Media, refused Alexander assistance. Problems continued well into 328, even after the capture of Bessos in Sogdiana (mid-summer 329).[31]

Alexander and Insubordination

Alexander's ultimate success can also be explained by the methods he used to break morale and military resistance. In the face of widespread revolts, he did not hesitate to inflict ruthless punishments on his opponents, both individually and collectively. The siege warfare mounted against the Sogdian towns was brutal. At Gaza, "on Alexander's orders, the Macedonians put all the men to the sword; and carried off the women, and children, and all kinds of plunder."[32]

The mobile columns that Alexander formed to speed up military intervention used similar methods. In response to the annihilation of a body of Macedonian troops in 328, Alexander acted as follows:

> Accordingly, in order that all who had revolted might alike
> be visited with the disasters of the wars, he divided his forces
> and gave orders that the fields should be set on fire and that

---

[31] A. B. Bosworth, "A Missing Year in the History of Alexander the Great" (*JHS* 101 [1981]: 19–23) is a detailed treatment of this episode.

[32] Arrian IV.2.4.

all who were of military age should be killed. (Quintus Curtius VII.9.22, cf. Arrian IV.6.5)

Alexander's aim was clear: to drive a firm wedge between Spitamenes and the rural population. And success was not long in coming: the next year, when news came of the Macedonians' approach, the peasants drove away Spitamenes' soldiers who had expected to be quartered in their villages.[33]

The picture we are seeing here is of a character very different from the "chivalrous" Alexander, whom ancient writers praised to the skies when he was fighting against Darius. But things had changed. Alexander's playing field was no longer an orderly, civilized arena in which he could display enormous urbanity and deep respect towards Persian princesses, and thus show up Darius's cravenness.[34] In rebellious Bactria-Sogdiana Alexander confronted battles, sieges, ambushes, and clashes at every turn, and he became increasingly irritated by the delays that this created for his Indian campaign. At the same time he knew that the ferocity of this war and the insecurity of their position as conquerors was affecting his troops' morale. What is more, this was no longer a regular war against a regular enemy, but one conducted against scattered rebel bands, whom Quintus Curtius significantly describes as "brigands" (*latrones*). Obviously we need to understand such terminology in the context of the ideological use made of it in the Roman era. It legitimized the actions of the conquerors, while belittling any who offered armed resistance.[35] When he left for India, Alexander knew full well that the submission of the two satrapies

---

[33] Quintus Curtius VIII.2.15.

[34] Briant, *Darius dans l'ombre*: 395–426.

[35] To suggest that Spitamenes and his associates were "terrorists" akin to al-Qaeda (as does F. Holt, *Land of Bones*, Berkeley, CA 2005: 51–52) is an anachronism, and, as such, should be firmly rejected.

remained precarious. To the slaughter, he now added the taking of hostages:

> To obviate any difficulties behind him that might interfere with his plans, he gave orders for 30,000 men of military age to be selected from all the provinces and brought to him in arms, to serve simultaneously as hostages and soldiers.[36]

He used the same tactic in India where, after the set battle against Poros, he again had to face massive uprisings. The campaign against the Mallians (326) was unusually violent. Arrian dwells on it at length (VI.6–14). In describing the satrap appointed when all the battles, sieges, massacres, and scenes of surrender were finally concluded, Arrian calls him "satrap of the surviving Oxydracians and Mallians" (IV.14.3).

According to Diodorus, he acted in much the same way in Gedrosia:

> There he divided his forces into three divisions. . . . He ordered Ptolemy to plunder the district by the sea and Leonnatus to lay waste the interior. He himself devastated the upper country and the hills. At one and the same time much country was wasted, so that every spot was filled with fire and devastation and great slaughter. The soldiers soon became possessed of much booty, and the numbers of persons killed reached many myriads. By the destruction of these tribes, all their neighbours were terrified and submitted to the king. (XVII, 104, 6–7)

The massacres and executions are a fact, but we should avoid the moral condemnation that can be readily found in the

---

[36] Quintus Curtius VIII.5.1, to which compare Arrian VII.6.1.

moralizing strain of Alexander historiography.[37] To say that "he spent much of his time killing and directing killing, and, arguably, killing was what he did best," is a sweeping judgment in harmony with our current values but not with those of Alexander's time.[38] Moreover, a critical reading of the sources suggests that the historian should be cautious.

To take just one example, let us examine what happened in one of the seven cities on the Jaxartes. Interestingly, Arrian clearly acknowledges in his account the contradictory statements contained in his two preferred sources, Aristobulus and Ptolemy:

> The seventh city he took without trouble. Ptolemy says they surrendered; but Aristobulus that Alexander captured this also by force, and slew all whom he found within it; but Ptolemy also says that he distributed the men among his army and ordered them to be bound and under guard till he should leave the country, so that none of those responsible for the revolt should be left behind. (IV.3.5)

There are two points to note here. First, as always, we must regard with caution ancient authors' accounts of rivers of blood and endless massacres. Here two informants, both of them eye witnesses, have provided contradictory information: according to one, Alexander puts all enemies in the city to the sword; according to the other, he takes them prisoner and adds them to his army; and what is more we later learn that some of them were eventually "redeemed" by the

---

[37] Rollin was, as far as I am aware, the first to declare (around 1730) that "Alexander doesn't scruple to sacrifice millions of men to his ambition or curiosity" (*The Ancient History*, trans. from the French, 18th ed., IV, London 1827: 365).

[38] The quote comes from Bosworth, *Alexander and the East*: V. Other statements by Bosworth could equally well be cited; cf. the title of his chapter 5: "The Justification of Terror." I have expressed my views on this current in historiography in *Studi Ellenistici* 16 (2005): 48–52 (with references).

king and installed in a new town.[39] Who knows which version is the right one? It is also important to be very wary of the numbers given, such as the "many myriads" killed (according to Diodorus XVII.104.7).

The second point to remember is that Alexander's decisions were obviously arrived at by taking into account both the decisions made by the foe (and vice versa) and the Greek "laws of war," as outlined by Xenophon (*Cyr.* VII.5.73), particularly those concerning encounters with "barbarians." Thus, if the enemy does not surrender voluntarily but offers armed resistance, then a general should feel himself fully justified in inflicting severe punishments, such as we see when considering the history of Greek cities in the classical period and throughout the Hellenistic and Roman periods. "Good" versus "bad" is not at issue here. These are wars of reprisal followed by counter-reprisals, and the booty taken serves the purpose of paying the troops. Alexander's behavior is thus fairly straightforward: those who surrender willingly escape with their lives,[40] those who resist to the bitter end, or refuse to supply the army,[41] run the risk of being put to the sword.

Further, the king was politically pragmatic. He did not massacre his opponents systematically; rather he used a range of available options: enrolling them in his army, taking hostages,[42] and/or granting pardons, even to groups who had rebelled twice over.[43] We are not dealing with an enraged and crazed (or drunken) megalomaniac, who orders massacres simply in order to calm his internal demons. This picture of a pragmatic Alexander runs counter to Plutarch's

[39] Quintus Curtius VII.6.27; cf. Briant, *Rois, tributs et paysans*: 244–47.
[40] See, for example, Diodorus XVII.103.8, 104.4, etc.
[41] *E.g.*, Arrian VI.21.3.
[42] *E.g.*, Arrian VI.14.3.
[43] *E.g.*, Quintus Curtius VIII.2.18–19.

highly dramatic depiction of an Alexander whose attack on the Cossaeans of the Zagros (324) is a "blood-soaked hunt," mounted "because of the anguish caused by the death of Hephaestion."[44]

The Discontent of the Macedonian Soldiery (330–324)

The difficulties of Alexander's position throughout this period were aggravated by the discontent of the Macedonian army, which never ceased throughout the campaign. According to Plutarch (*Alexander* 38.6–7), they first demonstrated their longing to return home on the occasion of the sack of Persepolis (spring 330):

> When the other Macedonians learnt the news, they came running joyfully with torches: they thought that, by burning and ravaging the Persian palaces, Alexander was showing nostalgia for his native land and his wish not to stay in their (sc. the palaces') midst.

A few weeks later the soldiers again showed their lack of enthusiasm, and this at the very moment when Alexander was trying to speed up his march in pursuit of the fugitive Darius. When they saw that the Greek contingents had been sent back, wild hopes sprang up in the army, which Quintus Curtius describes in a picturesque and moralizing style:

> As a result, gossip, the vice of idle soldiery, spread without authority that the king, content with what he had accomplished, had decided to return forthwith to Macedonia. They ran as though crazed to their tents and made ready

---

[44] Plutarch, *Alex.* 72.4; Briant, *État et pasteurs*: 94–100; note Bosworth's embarrassment, *Alexander and the East*: 145–46.

their packs for the journey; you would believe that the signal to march had been given throughout the camp. (Quintus Curtius VI.2.15–16)

After persuading the other officers to stand firm around him, Alexander called his troops together, and addressed them with a long discourse, in which he emphasized the uncertainties of the conquests already achieved. His arguments seem to have convinced the soldiers, who, according to the ancient sources, themselves urged Alexander "to lead them wheresoever in the world he wished" (Quintus Curtius VI.3.18).

The ancient writers do not make too much of this incident. Nevertheless, a series of internal conflicts suggests that, ever since his departure, Alexander and those close to him, on the one hand, and the mass of soldiers, on the other, had quite different ideas of what this enterprise entailed and, moreover, that Alexander had not divulged ambitions that might have alienated his soldiers and some of his commanders. The ferocious and inconclusive nature of the fighting in Sogdiana and Bactria sharpened the differences between Alexander and his retinue just at the moment when, for other reasons, a group of Macedonian nobles was expressing dissatisfaction with Alexander's manner of government.

When he heard that an entire contingent of his army had been exterminated, Alexander reacted in a way that shows very clearly the level of demoralization in the army:

With crafty prudence he concealed this disaster, threatening with death those who had returned from the battle, if they made public what had happened. (Quintus Curtius VII.7.39)

The weariness and low morale of the soldiers can also be attributed to the brutality of some of Alexander's tactics. Evidently the murder of Parmenion at Ecbatana in 330 by clandestine assassins acting on Alexander's orders had appalled the garrison soldiers to such an extent that a mutiny threatened. Alexander stooped to base treachery to identify and assemble the malcontents:

> Alexander selected from among the Macedonians those who made remarks hostile to him and those who were distressed at the death of Parmenion, as well as those who wrote in letters sent home to Macedonia to their relatives anything contrary to the king's interests. These he assembled into one unit which he called the Disciplinary Unit, so that the rest of the Macedonians might not be corrupted by their improper remarks and criticism. (Diodorus XVII.80.4)

Other writers specify that the king had himself urged his soldiers to write to their families, and that he had the packets of letters brought to him secretly.[45] In gathering these hotheads into a special regiment "the king's plan was to expose them to death or settle them in colonies at the end of the world" (Justin XII.5.8).

It is quite likely of course that the main cause of the Macedonians' discontent, particularly that of the more elderly, was that they were anxious to see their homeland again and to enjoy in peace the booty gathered in Asia. When Alexander ordered that altars be set up on the banks of the Hyphasis, indicating that he was not proceeding further, Koinos, the spokesman of the rank and file, expressed the exhaustion of the troops in a speech reconstituted by Arrian:

> Surely, you see yourself how many Macedonians and Greeks we were when we set forth with you, and how many survive. . . . The Greeks and the Macedonian forces have lost part of their number in battle; others have been invalided with wounds,

---

[45] Quintus Curtius VII.2.35–38; Justin XII.5.4–8.

and have been left behind in different parts of Asia; but
most have died of sickness, and of all that host few survive,
and even they no longer enjoy their bodily strength, while
their spirit is far more wearied out. One and all, they long to
see their parents, if they are still alive, their wives and children, and indeed their own homeland. (Arrian V.27)

Since 330, Alexander had been making ever greater
demands of his soldiers as he led them into increasingly hostile environments under climatic conditions that were as
unpleasant as they were severe in their extremes. During his
crossing of the Hindu Kush (329), snow blinded the men
and they were gnawed by hunger; the wounded and strag-
glers were abandoned on the side of the road.

The return journey from India, however, was based on
a fundamental misunderstanding. The soldiers were convinced that they would return to Macedon with the king at
their head, but this was not Alexander's intention. The
anger was immense when, at Opis (324), the soldiers no-
ticed "that Alexander was setting up the center of his kingdom in Asia for ever."[46] No episode better illustrates the
divergence between the ways in which the Macedonians
and their king viewed the conquest. It must have appeared
to the eyes of the plain soldiers that the king was preparing
to launch them into new schemes, enterprises of a personal
nature with which they themselves were decreasingly in
sympathy.

[46] Quintus Curtius X.2.12. On the attitude of the Macedonian soldiers by the
end of Alexander's reign and the beginning of the era of the Diadochi, see my remarks in Briant, *Rois, tributs et paysans*: 73–81.

Chapter IV

The Administration, Defense, and Exploitation of the Conquered Lands

When we look at the material that is available to us on the empire's administration and the policies Alexander adopted, we find ourselves engaging with a question that has been raised more than any other since antiquity. Was Alexander always led by the demands of war and conquest and by a taste for them, or was he also aware of the need to consider what Xenophon (*Oikon.* IV.4–25) called "the works of peace"? Xenophon created the prototype of such a ruler, a Great King who was as much concerned with maintaining peace and developing the prosperity of his lands as with provisioning his armies and garrisons.

And this leads to yet another question. Did Alexander expect, on his return to Babylon, to immerse himself (however briefly as it turned out) in the administrative and financial organization of the lands he had conquered? This question implies, of course, that in the preceding ten years he had been totally uninterested in these issues. The oft-repeated assertion that Alexander showed no interest in administration can neither be proved nor disproved. And in either case, it does not exclude the possibility that he was perfectly capable of making intelligent and considered decisions in this sphere.[1]

[1] See the highly relevant observations and analysis by W. E. Higgins, "Aspects of Alexander's Imperial Administration: Some Modern Methods and Views Reviewed," *Athenaeum* 1980: 129–52.

The Different Degrees of Royal Authority

In principle, all of the conquered territories were directly dependent on the king and his administration, and Alexander, always and everywhere, intended to exercise to the full the traditional monarchic rights over land and people.[2] This emerges from the terminology Arrian uses to describe the young Iranian recruits who came from Central Asia to Susa in 324:

> Then there came to him also the governors (*satrapai*) of the new cities which he had founded, and of all the spear-won land, bringing about thirty thousand youths.(VII.6.1)

When, after the victory at the Granicus, the king appointed a Macedonian satrap of Hellespontine Phrygia, he proclaimed his intention to retain "the taxes paid to Darius."[3] He maintained the same policy in his relations with the Greek cities of Asia Minor. His letter to Priene, however incomplete and vague in its meaning, makes his intentions in this regard perfectly plain. He distinguishes civic territory from the land worked by the local peasants (the *Myrseloi* and the *Pedieis*). While the citizens of Priene are exempted from the imposition of a garrison and the payment of a financial contribution (*syntaxis*), the village land is treated quite differently: "The countryside I decree to be mine, and those dwelling in these villages are to pay tribute." In other words, Alexander reaffirms his royal rights to land that he considers to be his, "royal land" inherited from the Achaemenids.[4]

---

[2] Apart from Berve's work (*Das Alexanderreich* I, Munich 1926), which gathered the evidence available at that date, consult Bosworth, *Conquest and Empire* (1988): 229–58 ("Alexander and His Empire"), E. Badian's article, "The Administration of the Empire," B1 (1965): 166–82, and the article by Higgins in the preceding note.

[3] Arrian I.17.1.

[4] The inscription has been frequently translated and commented upon; see for example, S. Sherwin-White, *JHS* 105 (1985): 80–87, the analysis by P. Debord,

Alexander's new administration, like the earlier, kept a close watch on the royal revenues, a large proportion of which derived from imposts on land, whose status in relation to royal authority varied enormously. In the short pseudo-Aristotelian work known as the *Economics*, which describes Alexander's kingdom (and implicitly the Achaemenid empire) schematically, the main job of satraps is collecting revenues, many of which are levied on the products of the land.[5]

But behind the principle of "the right to spear-won land" lies the reality that there was great diversity in the status and circumstances of the lands that had been conquered by Alexander. His march was extremely rapid, particularly in certain regions. He did not take the time to reduce the Achaemenid empire either systematically or in its entirety. The result was that the level of control varied greatly from locality to locality. In large measure this was a heritage of the Great Kings, who had allowed considerable local autonomy. The formula "dynasts, kings, cities, peoples," which nicely describes the diversity of Darius's realm, is also largely applicable to Alexander's empire. To simplify matters we will look at areas under two different degrees of subjection: regions administered directly by royal satraps and regions of "indirect government." The case of the Greek cities will require separate consideration.

The Satrapal Administration

Rather than examining one by one the twenty or so satrapies that made up Alexander's empire around 325,[6] we will

---

Asie Mineure (1999): 439ff., and my own observations in Briant and Joannès, eds., *La Transition:* 330–36 (with bibliography).

[5] [*Oikonomika*] II.1345b.

[6] Diodorus's list (XVIII.3) on the occasion of the division of satrapal commands in Babylonia in 323 is an adequate survey.

try instead to define the general principles that Alexander used in his administrative practice.

First, it is clear that he retained most of the Achaemenid structures, in particular the satrapies, the boundaries of which, with few exceptions, remained unchanged. One might have thought that the king would try to limit the power wielded by his own satraps, since his prime concern must have been to keep the empire united around him. But in this regard the evidence is contradictory. One reason for this is that the information assembled by the ancient authors came to them piecemeal and from different sources, which complicates the task of drawing firm general conclusions.[7] However, Alexander was a pragmatist skilled at adapting to circumstances he could not change. It seems very likely that the two nomarchs he appointed in Egypt in 332/1 (one was the Iranian Doloaspis, the other declined the position) held power in name only: Cleomenes, a Greek from Naucratis, was soon able to concentrate all civil power in his own hands and proved skillful at levying taxes.[8] And when Philip, the satrap of Taxila, was assassinated by his own mercenary troops, Alexander, then in Gedrosia, put in a protective measure that clearly demonstrates his flexibility:

> He dispatched letters to Eudamus and Taxiles bidding them take charge of the district formerly under Philip, until he should send a satrap to govern it. (Arrian VI.27.2)

[7] See for example on Syria and Cilicia, Bosworth's study, summarized in his *Commentary* I: 224–25.

[8] On the organization of Egypt, see especially Arrian III.5.1–7 (comparing it with the Roman administration of his own time), together with the comments of Bosworth, *Commentary* I: 275–78, and those of S. Burstein, *AchHist* VIII (1994): 381–87. On Cleomenes in Egypt, see the convenient discussion by Le Rider, *Alexander the Great*: 162–65 and 179ff.

Further, Alexander in several instances distributed satrapal powers among more than one officeholder. In Egypt
and the eastern satrapies that were under the control of an
Iranian governor, military power was vested in one or more
Macedonians. But this was not the case in the western provinces. There, the evidence shows clearly that the satraps
took military action throughout the period from 334 to 323.
The one exception is the special case of Caria where, until
around 326, the dynast Ada (who had adopted Alexander in
334) was given the satrapal title but not the military command. Alexander, with his well-attested pragmatism, left
military powers in the hands of the western satraps, knowing
full well that they would face chronic revolts and other acts
of insubordination from the people they governed, just as
they had in the Achaemenid period.[9] Dividing power in the
eastern satrapies, on the other hand, was sensible. There
Alexander's satraps would continue to exercise financial control, just as their Achaemenid predecessors had done;[10] the
pseudo-Aristotelian *Economics* shows that their chief task
was to levy the various satrapal dues.

The Macedonian satraps thus wielded considerable
power. How can this be reconciled with Alexander's concern to retain total control? The best explanation is probably that the dilemma never presented itself to him in quite
the juridical and institutional terms that exercise the historian. In the context of his conquest, he was well aware that
reorganizing satrapal powers would never, by itself, be sufficient to ensure the unwavering loyalty of his subordinates.

[9] See, for example, Diodorus XVIII.22.1 (the revolt of Laranda and Isaura against
the satrap Balakros, who died in the course of the fighting).

[10] On this (disputed) point, see my remarks in *REA* 74 (1972): 34–49 (= *Rois,
tributs et paysans*: 15–30), and most recently, G. Le Rider, *La naissance de la monnaie*, Paris 2001: 234–36.

Alexander's empire was in a continuous process of formation; it was an itinerant state moving forward in step with the movements of the conquering army. And it was this "itinerant state" that organized and oversaw the "sedentary state" that was being built behind it as the army advanced. This point is important: it was the presence (or absence) of the royal person that led certain satraps to obey or rebel, rather than the existence (or not) of intermediate structures for control.

The activities of some governors during the Indian campaign are a striking illustration of this. On Alexander's return, in Carmania, he dealt harshly with many satraps and administrators who had played fast and loose with their duties (making all sorts of exactions, usurping functions, etc.). Some authors (Schachermeyr, Badian) have even spoken of a veritable "purge," suggesting that in the face of a sequence of "conspiracies" Alexander unleashed "a reign of terror."[11] Such language is inappropriate: Alexander's personal position was never seriously threatened by anything so organized as a plot by a secret faction to undermine his power. Significantly, the main accusation Alexander leveled against his subordinates was that they "had not expected him to survive. . . . In fact, the satraps hoped that the Indian campaign would drag on; that Alexander would be overwhelmed by so many hostile peoples. . . . "[12] He wanted to act ruthlessly against "many of his officials who had used their powers arbitrarily and selfishly [and] had committed serious offences."[13] As Arrian (who, given his own position in the

---

[11] See Badian, "Harpalus" (1961 = B22, 2010) and "Conspiracies" (2000) in B14, pp. 50–95 (reprinted in B17, 2003, and B22, 2010), where the evidence is assembled; see the more balanced views of Higgins ("Aspects of Alexander's Imperial Administration: Some Modern Methods and Views Reviewed," *Athenaeum* 1980: esp. 140–52) and Heckel, B15 (2003): 210–25.

[12] Quintus Curtius X.1.7, and Arrian VII.4.2.

[13] Diodorus XVII.106.2.

Roman empire, must have been familiar with the problem) stresses, the king dismissed satraps and governors "who had neglected his orders" (VI.27.1), or "who were reported to him to be conducting [their] office in a disorderly manner (*ouk en kosmoi*)" (VI.15.3). Arrian uses this expression repeatedly when talking about the sacking of a bad satrap (VI. 27.3–4) or about the execution of generals who had abused their power by bullying the people under their authority:

> Both the natives and the (military) forces themselves brought many charges against Cleander and Sitalces and their followers of having plundered temples, rifled ancient tombs, and other overbearing and scandalous injustices (*adika erga*) to the inhabitants [of Media].

Faced with a situation of such disastrous dimensions, Alexander decided to have them executed. Arrian may have been influenced by the image of Xenophon's ideal monarch (*Cyr.*I.1–6), when he supplied the following simple and logical reasons for the king's policies:

> To put fear into any other satraps or governors who were left, that if they committed the like crimes they too should suffer the like fate. And this above everything else kept in order (*en kosmoi*) the populations which Alexander had subdued or which had surrendered to him, being as they were so many in number, and so far separated one from another— namely, that Alexander permitted no subject under his sway to be wronged by the rulers. (VI.27.4)

The very real fragility to which these affairs bear witness is a fragility that is known to all holders of personal power. In Alexander's case, everything was organized around his own person as the king. When he set out for India, he left no viceroy behind nor any kind of "prime minister," whose duty

73

it would be to keep watch over the satraps and punish their misdemeanors and attempts at extortion. He directed matters with the help of a mere handful of men, of whom only a few bore a title: the Greek Eumenes of Kardia was chief chancellor; Hephaestion, the king's closest friend, was given the Achaemenid title "chiliarch" and Harpalos (in the course of a somewhat checkered career)[14] was put in charge of finance. But these titles did not describe the holder's duties with any great precision. What mattered was the king's needs or inclinations at this or that moment. Eumenes' essentially civil function of chancellor-in-chief did not prevent him from participating in military action. And Alexander preferred to entrust occasional tasks ad hoc to the *somatophylakes* (bodyguards), about ten in number, whose allegiance to the king was personal.[15]

When Alexander had to deal with the situation he faced on his return from India, his natural reaction was not to introduce an administrative reform, but to replace the guilty with Companions in whom he had full confidence, and whom he knew would follow his orders to the letter. This allows us to pinpoint the Achilles' heel of Alexander's newly conquered world. Even within the directly administered lands, the unity of the empire was a notion linked more or less directly to the royal person. The actions of several satraps and administrators during periods of the king's

[14] See esp. Arrian III.6.4–7, along with Bosworth, *Commentary* I: 282–85, Le Rider, *Alexander the Great*: 204–5, and Badian, "Harpalus" 1961 (B22, 2010); on the title *hemiolios* (ps.-Arist., *Oikon.* II.2.34a), see H. Müller, "Hemiolios, Eumenes II, Toriaion und die Finanzorganisation des Alexanderreiches," *Chiron* 35 (2005): 355–84.

[15] For the terminology, function, and a listing, see W. Heckel, *The Marshals of Alexander's Empire*, London and New York 1992: 237–98; on fine distinctions and shifts in the hierarchy around the king, see the useful observations by the same author in "King and 'Companions'" (B15 [2003]: 197–210), and those of J. Roisman, "Honor in Alexander's Campaign" (B15 [2003]: 279–321).

absence—for example the extortions and flight of the treasurer Harpalos in 325—did not augur well for the future of the empire once Alexander was well and truly gone.

Areas of Indirect Government

Many territories were not subject to any form of direct administration but instead enjoyed a certain independence or effective autonomy, either because Alexander allowed them to retain a status that had been conceded or recognized by the Achaemenids or because the incompleteness of the conquest meant that satrapal control was a fiction. The status of the lands was thus diverse and variable, and could even be ambiguous.

Some regions were turned into satrapies without having been effectively conquered by Alexander. This was true of Cappadocia and Armenia. The former had merely lost a corner to Alexander in the course of his march in 333; the satrap (Iranian?) appointed by Alexander disappeared during the 333/2 Persian counterattack, and in 323, Cappadocia eluded Macedonian domination under the leadership of Ariarathes, who made formidable military preparations.[16] In Armenia, Alexander appointed an Iranian satrap, Mithrenes (the former commander of the citadel at Sardis), who was unable to take up the position because we know that in 316 the old Achaemenid satrap was still living there.

Other countries, theoretically incorporated into satrapies, continued in fact to be governed by their traditional leaders. This was true of Paphlagonia, whose sole obligation was to supply military contingents, and of Bithynia, which was able to preserve its independence in the face of the repeated attacks by the satrap of Hellespontine Phrygia.

Other regions remained *de iure* beyond satrapal influence.

[16] See in particular Diodorus XVIII.16.1–2.

Cyprus and Cyrene never formed part of the empire. The former retained its cities and kings, who had established good relations with Alexander.[17] Cyrene had sent an embassy to Alexander in 331 on the occasion of his journey to the oasis of Siwa; its relations with the king were defined by a treaty of alliance.[18] This explains why neither Cyprus nor Cyrene was included among the satrapal allocations made in 323 and 321. In Phoenicia, the cities kept their kings and institutions, although in Sidon Alexander replaced the pro-Persian king Straton with a more accommodating substitute, Abdalonymus.[19] The Phoenician cities were, however, obliged to contribute payments and to supply military contingents. In some respects their position was analogous to that of the Greek cities of Asia Minor.

In the Indus Valley, where satraps had been appointed,[20] the rulers who had been in place (including Poros) retained their authority at the local level. At the meeting in Babylon after Alexander's death, their status was confirmed, according to Diodorus: "Taxiles and Poros would remain lords (*kyrioi*) of their own kingdoms, as Alexander had laid down" (XVIII.3.2).

The Case of the Greek Cities

The Greek cities of Asia Minor "liberated" by Alexander, and the ones in European Greece, theoretically Alexander's

---

[17] The fleets of the Cypriot kings joined Alexander at Tyre: Arrian II.20.3.

[18] Diodorus XVII.49.2–3 ("friendship and alliance"); Quintus Curtius IV.7.9 ("friendship").

[19] On the romanticized history of Abdalonymus's accession, see the skeptical observations of S. Burstein, "The Gardener Became King—Or Did He? The Case of Abdalonymus of Sidon," in B18 (2007): 139–49.

[20] See Bosworth, "The Indian Satrapies under Alexander the Great," 1983 = B17 (2003): 170–77; K. M. Dobbins, "Alexander's Eastern Satrapies," *Persica* XI (1984): 74–108 (88–98).

"allies" as part of the League of Corinth, indisputably constitute one of the most ambiguous categories under his imperial administration. We saw that Alexander's behavior in the course of his campaign varied depending upon the attitude a city adopted towards him. But the real question is whether at some point Alexander promulgated rules applicable to all Greek cities in Asia Minor, or even indiscriminately to both those of Asia Minor and Europe. There are several aspects to this question. What was the relationship between the cities and the satraps? Were the cities in Asia included in the League of Corinth? There is equal controversy on both points.

When Alexander returned from Egypt in the spring of 331, he decided at Tyre to introduce a financial reform. Harpalos, who had fled before the Battle of Issus, was recalled and reinstalled in his position as controller of finance. At the same time, the task of levying the tribute (*phoros*) in Phoenicia was entrusted to Koiranos, and Philoxenos was given similar duties in Asia Minor.[21] Philoxenos's task was to collect the payments due from the Greek cities to support the "war of reprisal," with each city sending a few talents to the royal treasury. The same was true of the Phoenician cities, which were not under the jurisdiction of the satrap of Syria, but had to pay their tribute via Koiranos. In this way, two problems were solved: the system took care of the need for the king and his administration to monitor payments and channel contributions (*syntaxis*) and tribute (*phoros*); and the cities' civic autonomy was respected (including that of the Phoenician cities) since they were no longer directly dependent on the satrap. This arrangement lasted until the spring of 330, when the Greek contingents were sent home

[21] Arrian III.6.4; on this, see E. Badian, "Alexander and the Greeks of Asia," 1966 (= B22, 2010) and Bosworth, *Commentary* I (1980): 279–83.

and Alexander no longer demanded that the Greek cities make "voluntary" contributions. Nevertheless, Philoxenos retained the right to intervene in the cities should there be a threat to the Macedonian order. Throughout the period of Alexander's expedition, the theoretical freedom of the Greek cities was thus restricted, subject as it was to a superior authority.

The second issue, namely whether the Greek cities of Asia became members of the Corinthian League, is rather more complex. Some islands (including Chios and Lesbos) seem to have been members.[22] The extant documents do not allow us to decide the situation of the cities of the Anatolian coast. In the final analysis, the constitutional problem is probably rather less important than historians have thought it, given the fact that the League's powers and privileges were quickly reduced to token status. When Alexander left for Asia Minor, he entrusted the power to act on his behalf within the League to Antipater, his general in Europe. But in fact we know of only two actions taken by the League during Alexander's expedition. In 332, a rescript of Alexander regulated the situation in Chios,[23] which the Persians had reoccupied in 333 and put back into the hands of the oligarchs. One of the clauses of the rescript stipulated that those who had sided with the "barbarians"

> who have already taken to flight shall be banned from all the cities which participate in the Peace and be liable to arrest according to the decree of the Greeks. Those who have stayed behind are to be brought to trial in the Council of the Greeks.

[22] Cf. A. J. Heisserer, *Alexander and the Greeks: The Epigraphical Evidence*, Norman, OK 1980, and Bosworth, *Conquest and Empire*: 187–97, 250–58.

[23] Heisserer (see previous note): 79–95.

Then, after Antipater's victory over Agis III in 331, he left the fate of Sparta in the hands of the League. But it is worthwhile emphasizing the limitations of such interventions: the Chios rescript of 332 included clauses decided entirely by Alexander himself:

> Until such time as the Chians reach a settlement, an adequate garrison of King Alexander shall remain with them, and the Chians shall be responsible for maintaining it.

In 331, the *synedrion* handed the decision about Sparta back to Alexander—not surprisingly, as the members of the *synedrion* knew perfectly well that, ultimately, the League was little more than a convenient "channel of communication" for the king, who would in the end do whatever was most to his advantage.

A decision that Alexander made in 324 illustrates nicely his power to intervene in the internal affairs of the cities. During the celebration of the Olympic Games, his envoy Nicanor read a royal proclamation ordering the cities to recall their exiles.[24] This was an exceptionally important gesture, as the number of those banished in fourth century Greece was in the thousands. Reintegrating them caused major problems, particularly when it came to the disposition of their confiscated property. It is of little significance whether or not the royal rescript was formally in line with any of the articles of the Corinthian pact. The decrees subsequently issued by the cities show that they were applying

[24] Diodorus XVII.109.1, XVIII.8.2–6; Quintus Curtius X.2.4–7; Plutarch, *Alex.* 34.1; the relevant inscriptions are in A. J. Heisserer, *Alexander and the Greeks* (1980): 205–29; see also S. Dimitriev, "Alexander's Exiles Decree," *Klio* 86/2 (2004): 348–61 (who stresses that, in his opinion, several of the decisions emanated from the cities themselves); also Flower in B14 (2000): 126–28; Farraguna in B15 (2003): 124–27; Poddighe in B20 (2009), ch.VII.

the ruling in direct response to the royal order. It was this that had the force of law or, rather, it had the power to constrain the civic legislators. The pointlessness of trying to define the legal aspects of this rescript is made manifest by the fact that the king ordered Antipater to use force to compel any cities that refused to comply.

At this point, when Alexander was about to embark on new and far-flung campaigns (in Arabia), he wanted to make sure that the cities were internally stable, by removing "the various partisans in each city devoted to revolution and rebellion" (Diodorus). In this respect, his failure was total. Discontent was immense, particularly at Athens, which was already in uproar after the Harpalus affair. This situation must have been the chief reason for the violence and virtually unanimous rebellion that broke out in Greece immediately upon Alexander's death, although we know that it had been brewing in Athens for months beforehand.[25]

Territorial Control and the Management of the Population

The Imperial Order

The conquest of such a vast territory raised problems of policing. The ways in which the satraps of Asia Minor acted to "maintain order" illustrates the difficulties encountered by the Macedonians in controlling land and peoples *after* Alexander had left the scene. Particularly in Asia Minor, he had often done little more than accept a formal submission. Now, in order to protect the conquests already achieved, it

[25] Diodorus XVIII.8.2.

was crucial to maintain order in the subject regions, and this required making agreements with local dynasts. In this regard, the situation is comparable to that which prevailed under the Achaemenids, and indeed the Macedonians encountered failures whenever they tried to introduce abrupt changes to the basis on which collaboration between imperial authorities and local leaders was founded. This emerges particularly clearly in the case of the Uxians and Cossaeans in the Zagros, where Alexander's military offensives in 331 and 324 met with only short-lived success.[26]

Another major concern was protection of the strategic routes, which had to stay open to allow the Greek and Macedonian reinforcements to reach the theater of operations, and to enable armies on the move to locate the official supply centers en route.[27] We saw that this task was entrusted to the satraps in the western provinces and the military commanders of the eastern satrapies. To this end, each governor had an occupation force made up of Macedonians and Greek mercenaries, at least until 325, when Alexander decided that it would be wise to order the governors to dismiss the mercenaries they had recruited on their own initiative.[28] Some of these troops were stationed in garrisons within the satrapal capital, others in isolated fortresses or in the Greek cities.

Urbanization and Control of Inhabitants

In the East, urbanization—either in the form of true cities or of military colonies—was the chief means of ensuring the maintenance of Macedonian control of the regions so hard

[26] On this, see Briant, *History* (2002): 726–33 (with a map) and 1022 (references to my previous studies of 1976 and 1982, to texts, and an annotated bibliography).
[27] See ps.-Arist., *Oikonomika* II.2.38.
[28] Diodorus XVII.106.3, 111.1; cf. Badian, "Harpalus" (1961: 27–28) = B22 (2010).

won.[29] It must be significant that (with the exception of the Egyptian Alexandria) all the Alexandrias are to be found east of the Tigris. It is usual to think of these foundations as serving three different purposes: military defense, the settlement of nomadic groups, and the stimulation of economic activity, with all three goals sometimes combined in a single foundation. In fact, however, there is no proof that Alexander either planned or put into effect a policy of settlement in the Middle East. What is beyond doubt is that, *during* his conquest, Alexander's motives were essentially military, while some strategically placed towns were eventually to *become* commercial centers, a possibility he also envisaged. Alexandria-on-the-Jaxartes (Syr Darya), named symbolically the "Furthest" (*Eschate*), is a typical example, as Arrian suggests (IV.1.3–4):

> For the site seemed to him suitable for considerable development of the city; he also thought that it would be built in an excellent position for the invasion of Scythia; and for an outpost of the country against the raids of the tribesmen dwelling on the other side of the river. He felt also that such a city would become great both for the numbers of settlers and the splendour of its name.

Supervision of Sogdiana and Bactria was further secured by the foundation of another ten or so towns.[30] Similar concerns, in this case conflict with Arab neighbors, led to the foundation in 324 of two fortresses on the Persian Gulf at the mouths of the Tigris and Euphrates.[31] Further founda-

[29] Cf. Briant, *Rois, tributs et paysans:* 227–62; Bosworth, *Conquest and Empire:* 245–50; P. M. Fraser, *Cities of Alexander the Great*, Oxford 1996.

[30] The date of foundation and name of the city on the site of Ai-Khanoum (in modern Afghanistan) remains uncertain; for bibliography and discussion, see Fraser, *Cities:* 153–56.

[31] Arrian VII.21.3; Fraser, *Cities:* 168–70.

tions of fortified towns and other installations of garrisons are attested for India. Alexander also fortified the capital of king Mousikanos, because "its position seemed to him well suited for controlling the people living round about."[32] Similarly, Media was surrounded by "Greek cities to keep the barbarian inhabitants of the surrounding area obedient,"[33] and after his Cossaean campaign in the winter of 324/3, the king "founded substantial towns in the strongest places of the country."[34]

Conquest and "Economic Development"

Defining the Issue

While we can see how the lands and peoples were administered and controlled relatively clearly, trying to analyze the economic life of the empire is much more difficult. The ancient historians of Alexander had no real interest in such concerns, so that we are forced to glean whatever sparse items of relevant information are scattered through the narratives of conquest.

Understanding the economic aspects of the conquest is thus inevitably challenging, particularly as it is difficult to determine what Alexander's own thinking on economic questions might have been. Our conclusions will necessarily be linked to our image of the conquest: Was Alexander a "predator" or a "builder"? Was the new empire that we see rising from the still-warm ashes of the Achaemenid realm simply the result of an act of devastation, or should we see it as a durable structure? Was Alexander merely obsessed with

[32] Arrian VI.15.7; Fraser, *Cities:* 159–68.
[33] Polybius X.27.
[34] Diodorus XVII.111.6.

glory and victory, or had he considered what the consequences of his conquests might be? In other words, should
we see him as an adventurer and reduce his actions to instant responses to immediate needs, or as a true empire-
builder dreaming of the future that he was even now creating by building on the Achaemenid heritage? This is the
question that G. T. Griffith, more than forty years ago, considered to be both vital and unanswerable, namely:

> how far, if at all, Alexander changed the system which he
> found existing in it (the empire) already . . . [and] how far, if
> at all, Alexander was a man of reflection and a planner, and
> not predominantly a man of action in war and of improvisa-
> tion in the art of peace? (B2, 1966: IX)

Authors, past and present, have responded very differently
to these questions. Some think that Alexander never really
concerned himself with economic and commercial issues;
others, by contrast, have insisted that the conqueror had a
grand vision, which included this aspect of imperial administration. This was certainly the view of J.-G. Droysen, as
expressed in the first edition of his *Alexander der Grosse* in
1833. And the idea can be traced back further: from 1748 to
1757 it lay at the heart of Montesquieu's presentation of
Alexander's commercial policy, in particular his plan to
open a maritime route between the delta of the Indus and
the mouths of the Tigris and Euphrates.[35] As Montesquieu
saw it, Alexander's plan for expansion was accompanied by
his wish to create a close collaboration between Iranians
and Macedonians, both by means of intermarriage and by
giving Persian nobles access to positions of command. Furthermore, the peace and unity of the new empire was at

[35] Montesquieu, *De l'Esprit des Lois* (1757 edition), Book XXI, chs.VII–VIII.

stake. By a course that has not yet been completely charted, Montesquieu's ideas ended up three-quarters of a century later in Droysen's interpretation (although Droysen's vision is not precisely the same as that found in *De l'Esprit des Lois*).

In the wake of Droysen (1833), who was inspired by Plutarch, and as transmitted by Wilcken (1931), several writers present Alexander as a "grand economist": opening new routes, increasing agricultural productivity by means of irrigation, introducing a monetary economy (which they label "progress") in regions operating with a "natural economy" (which is equated with "stagnation"). This image of Alexander became the standard one for European historians and geographers of the interwar years, and elements of it are still with us today.[36]

In contrast to this view (on which Droysen's critics have been casting doubt since the middle of the nineteenth century) are those who condemn Alexander outright. According to them, he devoted himself unceasingly to war and conquest, indulged in massacres and destruction, and was quite incapable of administering an empire, except perhaps in the last years of his life on his return from India. This extreme view is rather less unorthodox than it seems, and is in line with the thinking of many historians according to whom Alexander was at bottom nothing more than a "predator." An eminent specialist recently ranged Alexander among those men of war who have ravaged the earth and massacred populations, leaving a trail of blood in their wake:

> For large areas of Asia the advent of Alexander meant carnage
> and starvation, and the effects were ultimately as devastating

[36] See my historiographical analysis in "Alexander and the Persian Empire, between 'Decadence' and 'Renewal': History and Historiography," in B20 (2009), ch.10.

as that of the Spaniards in Mexico. The conquerors created a desert and called it empire. (Bosworth B14 [2000]: 49)

From these responses, two contrasting images of Alexander again emerge: he is either a ravager of peoples and places,[37] or the "civilizing conqueror," bringing peace to the conquered, along with prosperity and economic development hitherto unknown under the "despotic government" of the Persians, and benevolently helping the "Orient" to raise itself to the level of the "developed" "Occident." We are left with the impression that we must choose between two Alexanders, each of whom is in fact constructed, explicitly or implicitly, in terms of the colonial and commercial history of Europe between the sixteenth and twentieth centuries. In essence, we are left deciding between a pro-colonial and an anti-colonial Alexander.[38]

This is an epistemological trap that the historian must seek to avoid. While we must of course read Plutarch's enthusiastic discourse on Alexander's "civilizing mission" critically,[39] we should treat with equal skepticism the condemnations poured upon him on the basis of our current values. Such judgments are pointless: instead we must try to understand what Alexander actually did in the administrative, economic, and monetary spheres.

Development and Exploitation

The first image that emerges from our sketchy documentation is that of a king concerned to explore the regions he is traversing and to note their levels of production. He wishes to draw

---

[37] E.g., Sancisi-Weerdenburg in B9 (1993): 185; Worthington 1999 (in B17 [2003]: 303–18); Brosius (in B15 [2003]): 172–93.

[38] See Briant, Rois, tributs et paysans: 281–90; "Alexandre et l'hellénisation de l'Asie': l'histoire au passé et au présent," Studi Ellenistici XVI (2005): 9–69.

[39] Plutarch, De Fortuna Alexandri, I–II.

up an inventory of the riches of the empire he is creating—
and not only of the treasures piled up in the royal and satrapal
residences, but also of the productive capabilities of the earth,
of what lies beneath it, and of the maritime regions.[40]

We know that Alexander sent out several expeditions
to the Upper Nile (Callisthenes), into the Persian Gulf (Archias, Androsthenes, later Hieron) and the Red Sea (Anaxicrates), and that he planned an expedition to the Caspian Sea (Heracleides).[41] But these were neither voyages of
discovery (Persians, Babylonians, and Arabs were familiar
with the Persian Gulf), nor disinterested scientific missions.
The task of those in command of the expeditions of 324/3
into the Persian Gulf was to make a report to the king about
the possibilities and problems of mounting a military expedition against the Arab coast:

> Then there was also the size of their territory, since it was
> reported to him the sea-coast of Arabia was as long as that
> of India, and that there were several islands adjacent and
> harbours all over the coast, large enough to give anchorage
> for his fleet and to permit cities to be built on them, and
> those cities likely to be rich. . . . (Arrian VII.20.2)

Such reports will undoubtedly have fed into the zoological
and botanical researches being conducted by the Lyceum
in Athens, such as the work of Aristotle's successor, Theophrastus (especially his *History of Plants*).[42] But was this

[40] According to P. Bernard (in *Travaux offerts à G. Le Rider*, London 1999, 37–
64), Menon accompanied Mithrenes to Armenia, and had been specially charged
by Alexander to take over the gold mines already exploited by the Achaemenid
administration.

[41] Arrian VII.16.1–4.

[42] In addition to the fundamental introduction by S. Amigues to the *Collection
Budé* edition of Theophrastus (*Recherches sur les Plantes*, t.V, Paris 2006: vii–lxvii),
see P. Fraser, "The World of Theophrastus," in S. Hornblower, ed., *Greek Historiog-*

really scientific exploration?[43] The documentation on this point is ambivalent. Take the example of the oxen captured after a victory in Swat (Gandhara), which were sent to Macedon:

> Thirty thousand oxen were captured and Alexander selected the finest oxen because he thought them of unusual beauty and size (*kaloi kai agathoi*) and wished to send them to Macedonia to work the soil. (Arrian IV.25.4)

Leaving aside the question of the reliability of the numbers given by Arrian, the text can be read in several ways. We can perhaps discern from it a leader anxious to increase the agricultural productivity of his kingdom. At the same time we might see in it the implementation of an imperial policy whereby the resources of one region (Gandhara) are used to stimulate productivity in another (Macedon) through the transfer of a previously unknown species of draught animals. We might also understand Alexander's decision as an effort at enriching Macedon by pillaging another region, in other words as an instance of a kind of plunder. Or we might also read it as, above all, an ideological discourse on the "good king," anxious to increase the wealth of his subjects, or for that matter as proof that, even at the furthest ends of the earth, Alexander never forgot that he was first and foremost "king of the Macedonians." Finally, it is conceivable that each of the above explanations illuminates one piece of a complex decision, known in a form elaborated by Arrian himself on the basis of sources that we are unable to identify.

---

raphy, Oxford 1994: 167–91, and D. Potts, *The Arabian Gulf in Antiquity* II, Oxford 1990: 129–38 (Theophrastus on Tylos/Bahrein).

[43] Cf. my observations in Briant, *Lettre ouverte à Alexandre le Grand*, Arles 2008: 127–32.

War and Peace: The Case of the Katarraktai of the Tigris

Because the rare nuggets of relevant information are so often embedded in a narrative context, it is difficult to distinguish "civil" from "military" aims in some of Alexander's enterprises. A striking instance is the removal of some structures erected by the Persians on the river Tigris. In February–March 324, Alexander sailed down from Susa to the head of the Persian Gulf, then moved up the Tigris, while Hephaestion was put in command of the land army. Arrian presents the king's decision thus:

> During this voyage upstream he removed the weirs (*katarraktai*) in the river and made the stream level throughout; these weirs had been made by the Persians to prevent anyone sailing up to their country overpowering it by a naval force. All this had been contrived by the Persians, inexpert as they were in maritime matters (*ou nautikoi*); and so these weirs, built up at frequent intervals, made the voyage up the Tigris very difficult. Alexander, however, said that contrivances (*sophismata*) of this kind belonged to those who had no military supremacy; he therefore regarded these safeguards as of no value to himself, and indeed proved them not worth the mention by destroying with ease these labours of the Persians.[44]

At first sight this passage seems rather anodyne; but in fact, it is extremely important. It brings us to the heart of the issue confronting us: the contrasting visions of Alexander

[44] Arrian VII.7.7; cf. Strabo XV.3.4, XVI.1.9. All the evidence is brought together and analyzed in my study, "Retour sur Alexandre et les *katarraktes* du Tigre: l'histoire d'un dossier I–II," *Studi Ellenistici* XIX (2006): 9–75 and XX (2008): 155–218.

that have been emerging ever since antiquity. For Arrian, as for Strabo, matters are plain and simple: Alexander is a reformer with a bold and lucid vision. He stands in contrast to the Persians who, unable to defend themselves against an offensive coming from the direction of the sea (the Persian Gulf), had placed barrages (weirs and dams) over the Tigris (as well as the Euphrates). They had thus blocked all maritime and riverine traffic between the Gulf and Babylonia. Alexander would set things to rights.

This view was first expressed in a report presented to Jean-Baptiste Colbert, the finance minister of Louis XIV, in 1667 and published in 1716,[45] and it has survived to the present day in the writings of Montesquieu, Robertson, Droysen, Wilcken, and many others. It has given us the image of Alexander as the "grand economist," a man anxious to stimulate commerce, to lift the "Oriental" world from its "Asiatic stagnation" to a higher "European" stage of development, converting a closed to an open economy.

These Western representations of the "benefits of colonization" in the wake of "the exploitation of land" appear even more convincing as the passage on the *katarraktes* of the Tigris is frequently linked to other information given by the same authors (Arrian and Strabo) about work ordered by Alexander in the following year on the Euphrates and on the Pallacopas canal. The actions he took are hailed as typical of "good leaders" desirous of "trying to assist the land of Assyria,"[46] and have traditionally been interpreted as proof of Alexander's interest in irrigation and the agricultural development of the region.

We thus see Alexander striving from the Tigris to the

---

[45] Cf. P.-D. Huet, *The History of the Commerce and Navigation of the Ancients* (English trans. of the Paris ed., London: B. Lintot, 1717).

[46] Strabo XVI.1.10 (*agathoi hegemones*) and Arrian VII.21.5–6.

Euphrates to boost the economic life of Babylonia. This is the most common view, based on an uncritical reading of the ancient sources. We should note that it sidesteps a major problem. Babylonia and Elam (Susiana) had been conquered by Alexander in the autumn of 331, and the king had appointed Iranian satraps—installing Mazday/Mazaeus in Babylon, and retaining Abulites in Susa. Why did they have to wait for Alexander's return in order to destroy these river defenses?

Alongside this, there is another view that runs in completely the opposite direction. It originates in an observation made by Carsten Niebuhr, when he was traveling in the Tigris-Euphrates valley in 1778. Drawing a comparison with the light barrages that he saw on the rivers, Niebuhr speculated that Alexander had destroyed barrages set up by the Persians in order to irrigate the adjacent land, "and not because they feared attack by a sea-borne power." This view was both supported and contested in various studies published from the eighteenth to the twentieth centuries, but had been largely forgotten when it was taken up as though it were self-evident by Schachermeyr in his monograph on Alexander (1949, 2nd ed. 1973). Bosworth has borrowed it, and presents it as support for his oft-repeated contention that the Macedonian conquest was a total disaster for those conquered:

> As he went he demolished the series of artificial cataracts which made the river impassable to navigation. It was the late spring, the river at high water, and water was flowing in torrents over the holding dams which in quieter seasons diverted some of the flow to irrigation channels. . . . Part of the motivation was certainly to prepare for the next year's offensive against Arabia, which would require an armada

91

from Mesopotamia, and Alexander was making the Tigris amenable to his purposes. . . . Alexander had no hesitation in destroying vital works of irrigation in the interest of improved navigability. . . . Nothing was to impede the passage of his fleets once the new campaign began. (Bosworth, *Conquest and Empire:* 159)

Again we find ourselves forced to make a simplistic and impossible choice. Did Alexander transform the conquered territory in positive or negative ways? Was he motivated by the requirements of his military project, or was he concerned to promote agriculture and commerce in the conquered lands? In my opinion these are false alternatives, based on a priori ideas about Alexander and on a faulty reading of the ancient texts, which ignores context and terminology.

If the *katarraktes* on the Tigris were not defensive structures positioned across the stream (against whom?), they were also not major irrigation installations permanently fixed on the riverbanks (holding dams). They were light structures made of earth, wooden faggots, and tree trunks that were put in place annually by the Persian-Babylonian administration when the river was low. Their purpose *was* irrigation, but they were removed at times of high water.

Alexander did what the Persians had done each year before him: he removed the *katarraktes* from the Tigris when the water was high, and, on the Euphrates, he closed off the emission canals and the overflow channels when the water was low (and opened them again at high water). To do this, he levied several thousand men by means of the corvée system, in accordance with a procedure well documented in the cuneiform record.[47]

---

[47] See Arrian VII.21.5: "Yet even so for three months over ten thousand Assyrians were engaged in this task." (Arrian expresses the number in myriads, which need not be taken literally.) On the corvées, cf. Briant, *History:* 401, 486, 933, and Kuhrt, *Persian Empire* II (2007): 708–11.

In my opinion, the conclusion to be drawn from this is self-evident:

> Alexander did not remove some useless riverine fortifications, nor did he wantonly destroy a system of barriers in place on the Tigris, which played a part in the irrigation system at the time of low water. . . . He was neither the "glorious" destroyer of a Persian defensive system, nor the "unworthy" devastator of a Babylonian irrigation system. For Alexander, the "work of war" and the "work of peace" went hand in hand; he conquered and managed his conquests. . . . In a country like Babylonia, he was well informed about the infrastructure of economic and social life of the cities and the organization of the great sanctuaries. Both his duty and his interest lay in the same direction, namely in maintaining the structures on the Euphrates and the Tigris, which made it possible, depending on the season, to avoid catastrophic floods and ensure the irrigation of the cultivated land. In sum, it is unnecessary to describe him as either a "grand economist" or a "civilizing hero"—simply, Alexander governed like a statesman, using the administrative traditions previously adopted and adapted by the Achaemenids, as well as introducing some Graeco-Macedonian innovations. He did not move like a predator through the countries and peoples as he pleased like an "Oriental despot"; he did not turn his empire into a desert, he had a vision for the future.[48]

If we turn Alexander's campaign into a simple pillaging operation, we forget that Alexander was not planning to drain or ruin forever the countries he traversed. He had a clear sense of the future of the empire that he was in the process of creating.

[48] I have here borrowed several sentences of the conclusion from my study, cited above: *Studi Ellenistici* XX (2008): 210–12.

Expeditions and Commerce in the Persian Gulf

What about another project attributed to Alexander: that of giving a new and decisive stimulus to trade between India and Babylonia via the Persian Gulf? That he had such a plan in mind is normally inferred from the expeditions he led by land and sea from the Indus delta.

We know that the return from India followed three separate routes. Craterus was ordered (July 325) to reach Arachosia following a northerly route (the Helmand Valley); Alexander himself used the coastal route through Gedrosia and Carmania; Nearchus, at the head of the fleet, was ordered to sail up the Persian Gulf along the eastern shore. Alexander's progress and Nearchus's must have paralleled each other. Alexander's main purpose was to locate the ports and establish them as depots of food and water, so that Nearchus's sailors would be able easily to get fresh supplies, as the coast was exceptionally inhospitable.[49] Nearchus's mission was not to undertake a complete exploration of the Gulf, but rather "to reconnoiter the coast lying on the Ocean, and the inhabitants of the coast, and its anchorages, and the water supplies, and the manners and customs of the inhabitants and what part of the coast was good for growing produce, and what part was bad."[50] At the end of January 324, Nearchus and Alexander met at the end of their journeys near Susa, and Nearchus made his report to the king.[51]

One year later, in Babylon, the maritime project was renewed and extended. A port was built capable of accommodating a thousand ships, and a fleet was constructed of

[49] Cf. Arrian VI.20.4–5; 21.3; 23.4–6; 24.3; cf. Bosworth, *Alexander and the East:* 166ff.
[50] Arrian VII.20.10.
[51] Cf. Arrian, *Indika* 42.

94

sections prefabricated in Phoenicia. It was carried overland to the Euphrates at Thapsacus and then brought down to Babylon, and the crews were recruited in the Phoenician cities:

> For Alexander had an idea of colonising the coast along the Persian Gulf, and the islands that lie near: for he thought that it would be just as prosperous a country as Phoenicia. His naval preparations were directed at the greater part of the Arabs, on the ground that they alone of the tribes on this side had sent no envoys, nor had done anything reasonable, or by way of honouring Alexander. The actual fact, in my estimation, is that Alexander was never satisfied in winning possessions. (Arrian VII.19.5–6)[52]

Arrian (VII.20.2–10) follows this up by remarking that Alexander was attracted by the wealth of this land, which produced all kinds of spices (myrrh, frankincense, nard, cassia, etc.) Moreover, its extensive coastline was well supplied with harbors and excellent ports, and was bordered by prosperous islands. All this was known to Alexander thanks to the reports that the leaders of his expeditions had made.

On the basis of these texts (Arrian, Strabo, and others), scholars have put forward the idea, ever since the seventeenth and eighteenth centuries, that Alexander planned to create an entirely new commercial network in the Persian Gulf. This idea, prominent in historiography from Montesquieu (1748, 1757) to Droysen (1833, 1877), was forcefully reiterated by Wilcken in 1931:

[52] On Alexander and Arabia, the special study by P. Högemann, *Alexander und Arabien* (Munich 1985) is interesting, but it is based on a notion, to my mind erroneous, of Babylonian "decadence" in the Persian period and its "renewal" by Alexander: cf. Briant, *History* (2002): 1019–20, and *Studi Ellenistici* 20 (2008): 179–89.

During his journey [from Pattala] and perhaps beforehand, Alexander kept in view the great plan of finding a way by sea from the Indus to the Tigris and Euphrates, and if he succeeded, of forming a connection between the western empire and his new colonial empire in India; not only would military security and administrative control be facilitated in his Indian possessions, but the trade of India would be connected with that of Hither Asia, and wide perspectives opened to world commerce throughout his Empire. (Wilcken 1967: 194)

Quite apart from the fact that this is a projection onto the distant past of a European model of military and commercial expansion, this perspective rests on two rather shaky assumptions: that commerce in the Gulf was nonexistent in the "dying" phase of Persian imperial history, and that the *katarraktes* of the Tigris (the Euphrates is generally added) had put a decisive brake on riverine and maritime links in the same period. But if, against this, we accept that the *katarraktes* were not permanent river dams, and that the Persian kings took a close interest in affairs in the Gulf, then a very different picture emerges. Following in the footsteps of his predecessors, Alexander conquered lands and seas that already had links with each other, and he planned to extract all possible profit from them. Despite the grandiose visions of Montesquieu, Droysen, and Wilcken, we can discern no trace of an "economic and commercial revolution."[53]

Alexander and Coinage

Droysen's commercial vision is mirrored by Alexander's production of coinage, which Droysen thought an essen-

[53] On this see my study, "Alexander and the Persian Empire," in B20 (2009): 171–88.

tial element of the long-term changes the king intended to introduce:

> One of the most powerful fermenting agents helping to create this new world must have been the immense mass of precious metals that the conquest of Asia had put into Alexander's hands. . . . When the new royal power which reigned in Asia now released these hidden riches, when it let them flow forth from its breast, like the heart pumps out blood, it is easy to understand that work and commerce began to spread them, with an ever increasing speed of circulation, through the terminally weary limbs of the empire; one can see how, by these means, the economic life of the peoples, from which the Persian domination had sucked the strength like a vampire, revived and prospered. . . .[54]

For some time now, the finds and analyses of coins show that, both in the short and long term, the matter is infinitely more complex. It is well known that the use of coined money was already widespread in the western lands of the Achaemenid empire before Alexander's arrival—in western Asia Minor, Cyprus, and Phoenicia. Darius I was the first of the Great Kings to mint coins, both in gold (darics) and silver (sigloi) bearing the image of the royal hero: dressed in the royal robe, the figure is shown as a warrior holding a bow and running, as though in pursuit of an enemy (Fig. 5). This royal coinage was struck in Asia Minor, predominantly in Sardis.[55]

When Alexander arrived in Asia Minor he was already familiar with the minting practices of his father in Macedon.

[54] The quote is from J.-G. Droysen, *Alexander der Grosse* (1833): 537; cf. my comments in the article cited in the previous footnote.

[55] On Achaemenid coinage, see the bibliography in Briant, *History* (2002): 934, and now esp. G. Le Rider, *Naissance de la monnaie*, Paris 2001: 123–238.

Fig. 5. "Royal Hero" on the obverse of an Achaemenid silver siglos, ca. fifth c. BC. Cabinet des Médailles (Paris), FG 126, all rights reserved.

For the time being, he did not try to impose a single imperial coinage to the detriment of the ones already in existence.[56] On the whole, the civic mints of the Greek cities of Asia Minor and of the Phoenician cities continued to function, with a few adjustments. Alexander did not open an imperial mint in western Asia Minor before 325/4. It is generally agreed that the minting of darics also continued in the eastern parts of the empire through his reign. What is more,

[56] See the fundamental study by G. Le Rider, *Alexander the Great*, which I have followed broadly in Briant, *Lettre ouverte à Alexandre le Grand*, Arles 2008: 135–45.

Mazday/Mazaeus, the Iranian satrap appointed by him, retained the right to strike coins in his Babylonian province.[57]

It was probably at Tarsus that Alexander decided to strike his own silver tetradrachms, which were very close in type to the coins issued there by the earlier Persian satrap, Mazday/Mazaeus. It is likely that the occasion for the first imperial minting of Alexander's Herakles and Zeus tetradrachms was the victory at Issus. A second workshop was opened at Tyre in 332/1, where gold staters with the images of Athena and Nike were struck.

If we accept these dates, the conclusion Le Rider reached in his study seems irrefutable:

> Thus, during most of the reign, in the areas of the empire west of the Tigris, apparently only two regions, Cilicia, Phoenicia, and Syria on the one hand and Macedonia on the other, produced the coinage that Alexander created after his victories at Issus and Tyre. The other areas, namely western Asia Minor, Egypt, and Babylonia, waited several years before undertaking their production. As for the eastern satrapies, from Susiana and Media to Bactria and India (satrapies covering a territory more vast than the rest of the empire), we have so far been unable to locate any mint of Alexander there.

> One conclusion is, therefore, compelling: Alexander did not mandate exclusive use of his coinage throughout all of his possessions. He took no all-encompassing measures. It follows that, in some regions, mints antedating Alexander's arrival continued to function, and that coins of local origin continued to be used almost everywhere, a point of view

[57] See the very full study by H. Nicolet-Pierre, "Argent et or frappés en Babylonie entre 331 et 311 ou de Mazdai à Séleucos," in *Travaux de numismatique grecque offerts à G. Le Rider*, London 1999: 285–305; on Mazday/Mazaeus's coinage, see my remarks in "The Empire of Darius," in B20 (2009): 162, 168–70.

that the contents of coin hoards confirm. (*Alexander the Great:* 254–55)

Further, it is wrong to think that the monetary economy reached the whole of the Near East and Central Asia all at once. As we have seen, the western lands of the Achaemenid empire were already enjoying the benefits of money circulation before Alexander arrived, and there is nothing to indicate that all the treasures seized by him from the great royal residences were turned into coin in the space of a few years. The proposed estimates of the weights of these treasures and those for the quantity of coinage minted by Alexander are far too speculative to provide a sound basis for judgment. In the regions (such as, in particular, Babylonia) where the preference was for using weighed silver, coinage developed only very slowly and never completely replaced the older system.[58]

We are very far indeed from the grand visions of Droysen and Wilcken! For Alexander, the unity of his empire did not mean the unification or homogenizing of monetary production and coin types. Instead, imperial coinages were produced concurrently with those of local mints. As under the Achaemenids, unity and diversity went hand in hand.

[58] See for example, Joannès in Briant and Joannès, eds., *La Transition:* 108–10.

Chapter V

Alexander among Macedonians, Greeks, and Iranians

In the rhetorical text he dedicated to Alexander's glory (*De Fortuna Alexandri*), Plutarch tried to account for Alexander's decision to adopt the Persian kings' official dress. His explanation is imaginative and rich in picturesque detail:

> When men hunt wild animals, they put on the skins of deer, and when they go to catch birds, they dress in tunics adorned with plumes and feathers; they are careful not to be seen by bulls when they have on red garments, nor by elephants when dressed in white; for these animals are provoked and made savage by the sight of those particular colours. But if a great king, in taming and mollifying headstrong and warring nations, just as in dealing with animals, succeeded in soothing and stilling them by wearing a garb familiar to them and following their wonted manner of life, thereby conciliating their rough natures and smoothing their sullen brows, can men impeach him? Must they not rather wonder at his wisdom, since by but a slight alteration of his apparel he made himself the popular leader of all Asia (*ten Asian edemagogese*), conquering their bodies by his arms but winning over their souls by his apparel? (*De Fortuna Alexandri* I, para. 8)

We may read in this passage Plutarch's response to contemporary writers who heaped blame on Alexander for identifying with the conquered and introducing Achaemenid court etiquette into his own entourage.

The eulogizing language of Plutarch's two discourses
On the Fortune of Alexander is certainly not the best introduction to the history of Alexander's relations with the
peoples of his empire—this despite the fact that it has inspired historians with its idealized portrait of Alexander
since at least the eighteenth century (*e.g.*, Montesquieu),
and particularly in the nineteenth (Droysen) and twentieth
(Tarn) centuries. Nevertheless, the passage is interesting because, aside from giving us the author's telling comparison of
the civilizing process with the taming of wild animals, the
text also illustrates nicely one of Alexander's tactics, namely
that of gaining the support of the elite of the empire he was
in the process of conquering. By "imperial elites" we should
understand the great Persian and Iranian families, who
formed the backbone of Darius's empire, as well as the leaders of subject communities.[1] This policy, which he deployed
deliberately and consistently, is one of the most crucial aspects of his strategy. His inspiration was the policy that had
been developed and used by the Great Kings themselves,
ever since the conquests of Cyrus.[2]

Conquest and Surrender: Contradiction and Opposition

The Imperial Elites vis-à-vis Alexander: From Sardis to Babylon and Susa

As we have already seen, military resistance to the Macedonian conquest was prolonged, recurrent, and tough, but it

[1] Schachermeyr's study of this subject ("Alexander und die unterworfenen Na-
tionen," B4 [1976]: 47–79) is very dated; the same is true of a very dubious article
by H. Berve, "Die Verschmelzungspolitik Alexanders des Grossen" (1938) = B2
(1966): 133–68.

[2] On the strategy of the Great Kings vis-à-vis local elites, see Briant, *History*:
79–84, 302–56, 800–813.

varied in its intensity and nature from place to place. Darius
and those around him were defending the principle of Achaemenid sovereignty, the tradition of the Persian people,
and the privileged place they held in the empire. But the
resistance of the Iranian nobility was limited by the fact that
their prime concern was to preserve their economic status
and prestige.[3] We can see an example of this in the summer
of 334. When Alexander reached the boundaries of Sardis,
a group consisting of local community leaders and Mithrenes,
the Persian commander of the citadel, approached him. The
former surrendered the city to Alexander, the latter the citadel with its treasury. We do not know why Mithrenes decided on this move at a point when Achaemenid fortunes
were far from decided, but we may assume that the surrender
was the outcome of negotiations with the conqueror. In return, Arrian tells us, Mithrenes obtained the following privileges from Alexander: "Mithrenes remained with him with
all the honours due to his rank."[4]

Here for the first time, Alexander deployed what would
become his standard policy: to rally the imperial elites to his
side by offering them the chance to maintain the status they
had enjoyed under the Persian king. He was well aware that in
order to govern the Persian empire in any lasting way, he would
need the support of the king's men, who alone could make it
possible for him to mould himself to the traditions of Middle
Eastern power. The case of Mithrenes shows that Alexander
had already devised his Iranian policy before landing. Arrian
adds that Alexander "allowed the Sardians and the other Lydians to retain their old Lydian laws and left them their free-

[3] For this topic, see the analyses and references in Briant, History: 842–44, 1046–
60.
[4] Arrian I.17.4 (the same expression is found at III.23.7); cf. Briant, "Alexandre
à Sardes" in B9 (1993): 13–28, and History: 842–43.

103

dom." In fact, Alexander did not change the existing situation in any way: Achaemenid Sardis was a fully organized community, under the control of locally elected magistrates.

Ancient writers stress that Alexander's task in Egypt and Babylonia was greatly eased by the fact that a large segment of the population perceived the Persians as oppressors.[5] But the image of "Alexander the Liberator" must be taken with a grain of salt. Although Egypt had indeed revolted several times and had even succeeded in gaining its independence between 400 and 343, it had certainly been in the interest of the elites to collaborate with the ruling powers.[6] The same factors explain their eager surrender to Alexander. Just as Cambyses and Darius I had done earlier, Alexander took pains to sacrifice to the traditional Egyptian deities, such as Apis in Memphis. He also journeyed to consult the Amun oracle at the Siwa oasis and gave orders to carry out work on the most prestigious Egyptian sanctuaries at Karnak and Luxor, where he was represented as a pharaoh (whether or not he was formally enthroned).[7] This, one would imagine, brought him the support of the most influential social groups: the priests and administrators of the temples. However, at the same time, "all activity dated by a ruler in this period need not necessarily have been done on royal initiative."[8]

[5] For Alexander's "triumphal" arrival in Egypt: Diodorus XVII.49.2 and Quintus Curtius IV.7.3; on the Egyptian responses, see Briant, *History*: 858–64, 1048–50; also 844–45 (Mazakes the satrap).

[6] See Briant, *History*: 472–84, 858–61, 948–50, 1048–50; for the Egyptian autobiographies, see most recently B. Menu in *Transeuphratène* 35 (2008): 143–63, with bibliography.

[7] On Alexander in Egypt and his insertion into the pharaonic ideology, see esp. B. Menu in *BIFAO* 98 (1998): 253–62, and S. Burstein in *AchHist* VIII (1994): 381–87. Burstein thinks Alexander's formal enthronement is merely a "scholarly myth" (*Ancient Society* 22 [1991]: 139–45); Menu (256–58) argues the contrary.

[8] Chauveau-Thiers, "L'Égypte en transition: des Perses aux Macédoniens," in Briant and Joannès, eds., *La Transition*: 375–404 (p. 377); on the works dated to

A stela from the Bucheum at Armant in the Thebaid reflects Egyptian continuities, as it mentions both Darius and Alexander. It is dated to Alexander Year 4, and mentions the burial of the sacred Bouchis bull born (probably) in the reign of "the King of Upper and Lower Egypt, Darius, may he live forever."[9] Of the three individuals mentioned—Darius, Alexander, and Bouchis—the only one to play an active role and have a real existence in this setting (albeit in death) is Bouchis. The two foreign pharaohs are simply named as chronological reference points. The document does not show that Alexander himself had given any kind of order relating to this ritual.[10]

The case of Babylonia provides some analogies. After Gaugamela (October 1, 331), Alexander was received with great pomp both by the Iranian officials (Mazday/Mazaeus and Bagophanes) and by the Babylonian authorities. A huge crowd, led by civil and religious authorities, came to hand over the city, the citadel, and the treasury, and Alexander, mounted in a chariot, made a triumphal entry into the city (Fig. 6). Here, too, continuities with earlier times are well marked. The victorious Cyrus was received with the same ceremonies in 539 and was portrayed as a liberator in contemporary Babylonian texts by writers who now served the new ruler (e.g., on the Cyrus Cylinder).[11] Yet Arrian (III.16.4) stresses that Alexander departed from the policy of his Achaemenid predecessors:

Alexander's reign, see *La Transition*: 390–93. For a different view, see D. Schäfer, "Alexander der Grosse—Pharao und Priester," in S. Pfeiffer, ed., *Ägypten unter fremden Herrschern zwischen persischer Satrapie und römischer Provinz*, Frankfurt-am-Main 2007: 54–74.

[9] See the references in Briant, *Darius dans l'ombre d'Alexandre* (2003): 63 and 562.

[10] Cf. Chauveau-Thiers, (n. 8, above) 377, n. 8, contradicting Van Voss in B9 (1993): 71–83.

[11] Cf. A. Kuhrt, "Alexander in Babylon," *AchHist* V (1990): 121–30.

Fig. 6. The Persian Mazday (Mazaios) advances to receive Alexander at the gates of Babylon. Mazday (at left) is preceded by Peace (the winged goddess) and by his five sons. Engraving from *Bas-reliefs de Albert Thorwaldson I: Entrée d'Alexandre à Babylone en 18 planches, gravées d'après les dessins de Fr. Overbeck à Rome, d'après les dessins de P. Bettelini et D. Marchetti, et publiés par Ch. Jugel à Francfort/Main* 1838, Pl. 17.

On entering Babylon, Alexander directed the Babylonians to rebuild the temples Xerxes had destroyed, and especially the temple of Bel, whom the Babylonians honour more than any other god.

That there had been revolts against Xerxes is beyond doubt, and these had certainly had consequences in Babylonia. However, the destruction of temples attributed here to the Great King and his "intolerance" rest on a very fragile basis—a tradition largely constructed to emphasize, by contrast, Alexander's good qualities and popularity. What is undoubtedly true is that Alexander, like his Persian predecessors, took care to obtain the blessings of the local gods. The support of city and temple governors made it possible for him to impose his rule using the traditions of Babylonian kingship, by adopting its titles ("King of Lands") as the Persian kings had done.

This cooperation between conqueror and conquered was not based on an enthusiastic and spontaneous reception offered by the latter to the former, but on an agreement drawn up after the Battle of Gaugamela. This is shown quite unambiguously by a now-famous astronomical text that clearly alludes to the period following Darius's defeat at Gaugamela and Alexander's entry into Babylon.[12] Neither the classical nor the Babylonian texts give us any direct information on what Babylonians of diverse social standing might have felt. However, it is probably fair to say that the classical writers have a tendency to exaggerate their enthusiasm for the events of 331 and to express more hostility for those of 324/3,[13] while, to use R. Van der Spek's expression, "the opinion of the Babylonian population remains a mystery for us." Nevertheless, it is clear that the community of interest between Persian rulers and the leading segments of Babylonian society was so strong that it was unlikely to vanish from one day to the next. In short, whether we are talking about Egypt or Babylonia, Alexander did everything he could to adopt the ideologies of Eastern conquerors, who presented themselves regularly as benefactors of the sanctuaries in the countries over which they had just established their power, in contrast to the rulers who preceded them.

The Persepolis Affair

Alexander's ideological strategy of winning over local aristocracies was developed and applied from 334 on. When this pragmatic policy is set alongside his decision to destroy Persepolis in May 330, the historian is faced with an obvious paradox.[14] Several explanations have been advanced, but the problem lies in determining which is the decisive one.

[12] For the text, see R. Van der Spek, in *AchHist* XIII (2003): 297–99 and A. Kuhrt, *Persian Empire* I (2007): 447–48.

[13] See, for example, Arrian VII.17.3–4 with the commentary of Van der Spek in Briant and Joannès, eds., *La Transition*: 269–71 and *AchHist* XIII (2003): 332–42.

[14] The bibliography on this is gigantic; it is partly cited and commented in Briant, *History*: 850–52, 1046–48.

The decision is difficult. The literary tradition (with the exception of Arrian, who is very succinct) is very voluble in describing the scene, but virtually silent on the sentiments of the inhabitants of Persis, while the archaeological publications are very incomplete and it is, in any case, not possible for them to provide the definitive conclusions that we seek.[15]

In order to avoid any misinterpretations and errors, we need to distinguish three phases, different in kind and importance:

(i) first, soon after the surrender of the city and the citadel (end of December 331–January 330), the soldiers looted the private houses[16] and Alexander seized the treasury (phase A);[17]

(ii) next, four months later (May 330), Alexander ordered certain official buildings on the terrace to be burned[18] (phase C);

(iii) during an intervening phase B there occurred events and episodes reported or referred to in passing by Diodorus and Quintus Curtius that may help us to understand why and how, in the space of four months, Alexander reached the decision that initiated phase C.

Phase A does not pose any particular problems; looting (the soldiers' booty) and the seizure of treasures (the king's share) are common acts of war. Diodorus's and Quintus Cur-

---

[15] See the essays on this by Hammond (1992 = B11, II [1997]: 233–34), Sancisi-Weerdenburg (B9 [1993]: 177–88), and Bloedow-Loube, *Klio* 79/2 (1997): 341–53.

[16] Diodorus XVII.70.2–6 and Quintus Curtius V.6.8; omitted by Arrian and Plutarch.

[17] Arrian III.18.10, Plutarch, *Alex.* 37.4, Diodorus XVII.71.1–2, Quintus Curtius V.6.9–10.

[18] Arrian III.18.11 ("The Persian palace he set on fire"), Diodorus XVII.72, Quintus Curtius V.7.1–8, Plutarch, *Alex.* 38.

tius's lengthy literary descriptions were intended to excite feelings of pity among their Greek and Roman readers,[19] but they do not allow us to conclude that the brutality of the pillage was exceptional.[20] The deliberate burning of the palace (phase C), however, raises obvious problems. Why did Alexander take this decision to demonstrate that Darius's power was in all respects null and void, when his prime objective was to bring the Persian and Iranian nobility over to his side? At first, his campaign of persuasion looks as though it was fairly successful: the commanders of Persepolis (Tiridates) and Pasargadae (Gobares) opened their gates to him, and they were duly rewarded by their new master.

It is difficult to believe one of the old traditions (although it is often repeated); namely, that the burning of the palaces was decided on under the influence of drink, in the context of the war of reprisal (symbolically represented by the Athenian courtesan Thais). A different and more credible tradition suggests, by contrast, that the decision was the result of long deliberation. Alexander's later regrets show that it was a difficult one and that he was clearly aware of the political implications and the dubious logic of the act. The destruction of Persepolis (as Arrian expresses it in the person of Parmenion)[21] amounted "to destroying what was now his own property." Above all it risked alienating the leading Persians whom Alexander was anxious to recruit, as well as seriously weakening his position and his ideological status at a moment when the real Achaemenid, Darius III,

---

[19] See also Quintus Curtius V.5.5–24; Diodorus XVII.69.2–9: the "moving" description of the Greek deportees at Persepolis.

[20] The term "hooliganism" used by Brosius (B15 [2003]: 183) is completely inappropriate; the same goes for the expression "ground zero" used by Lane Fox (in C. Tuplin, ed., *Persian Responses*, Swansea [2007]: 276).

[21] Arrian III.18.11; for the literary construction of "Parmenion" in Arrian, see E. Carney in B14 (2000): 263ff.

had certainly not abandoned hope of reversing the military situation but was in fact gathering new forces in Median Ecbatana.

Did Alexander wish to please the Greeks and send them a "signal"? This suggestion is based in large part on a synchronism established (or rather proposed by scholars) between Alexander's decision in Persis and the news of Agis's revolt and his defeat by Antipater's troops. Neither of these suggestions is very convincing.[22] For one thing, phase A (the looting and appropriation of the treasures on the terrace) was in itself a very clear act of revenge. For another, the "war of reprisal" was not the king's chief preoccupation in the spring of 330. A variant theory has been proposed, namely that the king wished to send a message to the peoples of the Middle East, inasmuch as burning the palaces at Persepolis removed a symbol of Achaemenid imperial domination. But which populations do we mean? Neither Egypt nor Babylonia nor any of the other great states of this region posed, at that point, any major threat in terms of maintaining control. All things considered, the need to send out a positive message to Greece and/or the inhabitants of the Middle East could not have been so pressing as to justify the risk of alienating the Iranian nobility.

It is more likely that the full historical significance of the events in the spring of 330 should be understood in a purely Persian context (taking "Persian" in its narrow sense). Let us consider phase B. During the four months between his arrival in Persia and the burning of the palaces (January through May of 330), Alexander had tried both to put down

[22] See above all Badian, "Agis," in: I. Worthington, ed., *Ventures into Greek History*, Oxford 1994: 258ff., esp. 281–92, but the arguments put forward remain weak, whether they concern Alexander's isolation at this time (pp. 285–89) or the awkward observations on the date of Agis's death (pp. 272–77, 291). On all these issues, E. N. Borza's studies (*Makedonika* 1995: 201–210, 217–38) are to be preferred.

military resistance in the countryside and in the strongholds in Persis, and to woo its inhabitants to his side. And he did not stint in his efforts. Although the edifying stories of his desired link with the memory of Cyrus the Great may date from his second visit to Pasargadae on his return from India, it is still likely that from 330 onwards Alexander showed his respect for the tomb of Pasargadae's founder, where the traditional sacrifices were continued under the new regime.[23] If the decision to burn the palaces was taken soon after Alexander's return from Pasargadae, it simply shows that his piety toward Cyrus's tomb had not diminished Persian hostility, as Diodorus and Quintus Curtius make plain.[24] Under these circumstances Alexander decided to have recourse to the force of arms to impress the Persian population, which continued to be recalcitrant. The burning of the palaces was a signal to the Persians that their days of imperial glory were over, unless they came over to the side of the conqueror. The price Alexander paid for this demonstration was heavy, but he had no choice.

The Use of Iranians in the Administration and the Army

Alexander continued his campaign against Darius, but he did not abandon his project of recruiting the Iranian nobility—quite the contrary. Studying the relations between conquerors and conquered is a complex business: social, regional, and chronological subtleties need to be taken into account. Not all the standard-bearers of the Achaemenid order put up a

[23] On the sacrifices at the tomb of Cyrus, cf. Briant, *History*: 95–96, 895.

[24] Diodorus XVII.71.3, Quintus Curtius V.7.2, and Briant, *History*: 850–52, 1046–47. The Sassanian and Arab-Persian texts are not to be included in this discussion (despite, *e.g.*, Shahbazi, "Iranians and Alexander," *AJAH* n.s. 2/1 [2003]: 5–38), as these later reconstructions are not based on any independent evidence of what actually happened in Alexander's lifetime (cf. Briant, *Darius dans l'ombre*: 443–86).

Figure 7: The tomb of Cyrus the Great at Pasargadae, sixth century BC. Photo: copyright Pierre Briant.

sustained ideological resistance to Alexander. The aristocratic Persian caste, anxious to preserve its economic and social power, joined him fairly swiftly. The situation was the same in Eastern Iran (Bactria and Sogdiana).

The burning of Persepolis thus did not mark a brutal and decisive turning point in Alexander's ideological strategy. The murder of Darius III by Bessos and his accomplices in July 330 was a gift to Macedonian propaganda, and henceforth Alexander cast himself in the role of Darius's rightful avenger.[25] He certainly never recognized Bessos's proclamation of himself as king with the name Artaxerxes, and the campaign he conducted against Bessos was, according to Macedonian propaganda, a veritable war of vengeance. In this way, he hoped to gather around himself the Iranian aristocracy, who had always constituted the backbone of the

[25] But the return of Darius's corpse to Persepolis (Arrian III.22.1) remains doubtful, for reasons explained elsewhere (Briant, *Darius dans l'ombre*: 39–52).

Great King's empire. It was a risky policy: several Iranians had ulterior motives; some took up arms to Alexander's rear in support of Bessos, thus obliging the Macedonian king to halt his direct offensive against Bactria.

We have already seen that Alexander had in mind this policy of inclusion as early as his entry into Sardis in the summer of 334. Yet the Persian Mithrenes had not been given a high-level post in the imperial administration; such posts were reserved for Greeks and Macedonians. Alexander's entry into Babylon (October 331) clearly marked an important turning point. For the first time, Alexander installed a Persian satrap (Mazday/Mazaeus) in a newly conquered satrapy (Babylonia).[26] Afterward, other members of the old governing class were appointed—and in large numbers—in Susa, in Persepolis, and in the provinces of the Iranian Plateau. Of the twelve satrapies conquered and reorganized between 331 and 327, only one, Arachosia, was given to a Macedonian (Menon); all the others were, at least initially, bestowed on Iranians.[27]

In doing this, Alexander demonstrated his awareness of the realities he faced. He granted a pardon to every Persian administrator who submitted to him, even the former chiliarch Nabarzanes, who had plotted with Bessos. The result was that several Persian satraps remained in their posts, at least for the time being, including Abulites and Oxathres in Susiana, Aspates in Carmania, Autophradates among the Tapurians and Mardians, and Satibarzanes in Areia-Drangiana. Others were swiftly recalled to their old positions, such as Atropates to Media in 328/7 and Phrataphernes to Parthia-

[26] On Mazday/Mazaeus, see Briant, "Empire of Darius III," in B20 (2009): 160–62, 168–70.

[27] For a list of satraps and satrapies, see Berve, *Alexanderreich* I (1926): 253–73, and the biographical notes in W. Heckel, *Who's Who in the Age of Alexander* (2006); see also Brosius in B15 (2003): 188–92 (whose conclusions I do not share).

Hyrcania after 330. It would appear that one of Alexander's major concerns was to ensure administrative continuity.

It should be stressed, at the same time, that the king took every precaution to ensure that the Iranian governors remained loyal. First, several had been in his entourage for some years. This is true of Mithrenes, who was appointed governor of Armenia in 331 (but was never able to take control) and had been with Alexander since handing over the citadel at Sardis in summer 334. Others had been in exile for a while at the Macedonian court, among them Amminapes and Artabazus (who was installed in Bactria).[28] There is further the case of Oxyartes, Alexander's father-in-law, whose daughter Roxane served, to some degree, as a guarantee of her father's loyalty. Clearly, Alexander did not entrust his satrapies to strangers. Furthermore, these satraps did not have military powers, apart from Menon in Arachosia who was a Macedonian. This was already the arrangement established in Egypt, where all military positions were in the hands of Macedonians.[29] A Macedonian general in command of the occupation forces resided in each province. Another point to note is that in the course of the conquest the number of Iranian satraps declined steadily. In Areia, the rebellious satraps Satibarzanes and Arsakes were replaced by the Greek Stasanor, and in 328 he also received the Tapurian-Mardian province, whose governor Autophradates had tried to secede. In Bactria, the aged Artabazus had to cede his position to the Macedonian Amyntas in 328/7. In fact, by the time Alexander set off for India, the most strategically important satrapies were in the hands, either directly (Bactria, Sogdiana, and Arachosia) or indirectly (Media and

---

[28] On Artabazus and the history of his family, see Briant, *Lettre ouverte à Alexandre le Grand*, Arles 2008: 151–58.
[29] Arrian III.5.2–7.

Parapamisadae), of Macedonians or of Iranians whose loyalty was in no way suspect (Mazday/Mazaeus, for example, who kept the satrapy of Babylonia down to his death in 328).

The same pragmatism and prudence guided Alexander's decision to enroll Iranian military contingents.[30] The guerilla tactics Alexander encountered in eastern Iran showed plainly that he would have to adopt the equipment and methods of his opponents. Accordingly, he recruited a corps of infantry and mounted archers (*hippotoxotai*), who amply proved their worth during the Indian campaign. General manpower was also in short supply. Despite the continuous influx of Macedonian reinforcements and Greek mercenaries, Alexander found that he needed ever larger numbers of infantry and cavalry soldiers. Thus he recruited contingents of horse in Sogdiana and Bactria, regions justly famous for their cavalry. We should note, however, that this corps served in an auxiliary role and was not integrated into the Macedonian army until the return from India. The Macedonian cavalry never lost its unique status as a part of the victorious army.

Alexander's decision to recruit 30,000 young Iranians in the eastern satrapies was also taken just before his departure for India (probably in Bactria). They were obliged to learn Greek and to train in the Macedonian manner. According to Quintus Curtius (VIII.5.1), these young men should be regarded as hostages held by Alexander. In the short term this is a valid analysis, at least in part. The king wanted to be sure that the satrapies, which had been so hard to conquer, remained quiet during his absence. But in the mid- to long-term, Alexander undoubtedly had a larger and

---

[30] On the growing but gradual introduction of Iranian troops, see A. B. Bosworth, "Alexander and the Iranians" (1980 = B17 [2003]: 208–35; also, Bosworth, *Conquest and Empire*: 271ff). However, I do not share all the author's minimalist views of Alexander's policy.

more positive vision, namely, to create, almost certainly on the basis of an Achaemenid institution, a new army corps, which would in time be incorporated into the phalanx.[31]

Marriage and Colonization

In the years to come Alexander's policy with regard to those he had conquered would evolve even further. His most spectacular gesture was his marriage to Roxane, daughter of the Iranian noble Oxyartes, who had been leading the resistance of "the Sogdian Rock" (spring 327).[32] What motivated Alexander? While the possibility of "love at first sight" cannot be discounted, the ancient authors make it plain that the marriage was politically motivated. Marrying Roxane was a decisive step in securing the direct collaboration of the Persian and Iranian nobility. His father-in-law Oxyartes was appointed satrap of the Parapamisadae. The union with the Sogdian family immediately brought the Iranian nobility onto his side inasmuch as it could be seen (and rightly so) as proof of Alexander's lasting involvement with the local aristocracies. Moreover, several of his Companions followed in Alexander's footsteps, taking local brides.

At the same time, this policy exacerbated opposition from part of the Macedonian nobility, who suspected that Alexander was planning to identify himself with the Iranian nobility. The evidence, however, suggests otherwise. Contrary to what is often said, the marriage rite picked for the ceremony was not Iranian, but Macedonian.[33] This is re-

[31] See P. Briant, "The Achaemenid Empire," in K. Raaflaub and N. Rosenstein, eds., *Soldiers, Society and War in the Ancient and Medieval Worlds*, Cambridge, MA 1999: 105–28.

[32] Sources, bibliography, and interpretations in E. Carney, *Women and Monarchy in Macedonia*, Norman, OK 2001: 82–113, and B15 (2003): 242–52.

[33] Cf. M. Renard and J. Servais, "À propos du mariage d'Alexandre et de Roxane," *Antiquité Classique* XXIV (1955): 29–50.

vealing: it was not for the Macedonians to give up their identity, but for the Iranians to adopt Macedonian custom. The recruitment of the 30,000 Iranian soldiers (training in the Macedonian manner and learning Greek) was a step in the same direction.[34]

In this same period the policy of colonization and urbanization, which was to have such important consequences, was inaugurated and actively pursued.[35] The new foundations were virtually always settled with a mix of peoples: Macedonian veterans, Greek mercenaries, and locals. According to Arrian, all were volunteers. But it is doubtful whether the local people were taken from their traditional villages, as had been done in the case of Alexandria in Egypt and Alexandria on the Tigris or Gaza (Phoenicia). In the case of Alexandria on the Jaxartes, they were prisoners-of-war redeemed (!) by Alexander, and they were certainly not in a position to choose.[36] The same is true of Macedonians in several instances. Thus, in 330, soldiers of the "insubordinate battalion" were deported to far-distant garrisons, and it goes without saying that Alexander did not ask for their opinion.[37] The reactions of the Greek mercenaries show plainly, right from the start, that their settlement was not voluntary: they rebelled several times while Alexander was in India.[38] In spite of the measures he took on his return, trouble continued. After Alexander's death in 323, things

[34] Arrian VII.6.1.

[35] On this theme, see Bosworth, *Conquest and Empire:* 245–50 and Fraser, *Cities of Alexander the Great* (1996): 171–90.

[36] Arrian IV.4.1 (cf. IV.27.1, V.29.3); cf. Briant, *Rois, tributs et paysans:* 244–47, 253, and "Colonizzazione ellenistica e popolazioni del Vicino Oriente: dinamiche sociali e politiche di acculturazione," in S. Settis, ed., *I Greci* 2/III, Turin 1998: 309–33.

[37] Cf. Justin XII.5.8.

[38] See Quintus Curtius IX.7.1–12 and Diodorus XVII.99.5 (much romanticized); cf. Arrian V.27.5.

were so bad that an army had to be sent against them, result-
ing in the extermination of several thousand Greeks who
had taken up arms. There was also a revolt by Greek mercenaries in India, after Alexander had left, in which the Macedonian satrap of Taxila lost his life.

Alexander's method of colonization was only very re-
motely comparable to Isocrates' ideas. When Isocrates suggested that colonies be founded for poor Greeks, he was
thinking of Asia Minor, not of the eastern satrapies. The
Greek colonists who rebelled were homesick, like the Macedonian soldiers on the Hyphasis or at Opis. "They longed for
the Greek customs and manner of life (*hellenike agoge kai
diaita*), and were relegated to the far bounds of the empire."[39]
Further, colonization in the Greek sense presupposed the
distribution of land parcels and the establishment of Greek
institutions for internal government (deliberative assem-
blies, elected magistrates, etc.). But, as we have already observed, most of Alexander's foundations were not strictly
speaking cities. Furthermore the ancient texts show that the
Greeks were vigorously opposed to any policy of fusion. Although Alexander's aim was primarily motivated by military
considerations, it is nevertheless the case that these foundations led to unions between European colonists and local
women, as the Greeks and Macedonians could not normally
bring their wives with them.[40] The status of the children
born from these unions was a problem. When the veterans
returned to Macedon (323), they left several thousand children behind, whom the king promised to bring up and arm
"in the Macedonian manner."[41] These examples show the

[39] Diodorus XVIII.7.1 (cf. XVII 99, 5–6); cf. Briant, *Rois, tributs et paysans:* 73–81.
[40] See Arrian VII.5.8: ten thousand of Alexander's soldiers married women in
the conquered lands.
[41] Arrian VII.12.1–2.

limits of fusion, which it would be more appropriate to dub "assimilation," and which tended to preserve the preferential status of the victors. We must recognize also that Alexander encountered strong resistance from Greeks and Macedonians in trying to implement his policy.

Macedonian and Personal Kingship: The Macedonian Opposition

It was in the same period that the so-called three "catastrophes" occurred (330–327), which clearly revealed the opposition of an important section of the Macedonian nobility to the changes they saw taking place in their king. First, the trial and execution of Philotas (autumn 330), then the murder of Kleitos (winter 328/7), and finally the *proskynesis* affair and the arrest of Callisthenes (327).[42] In order to grasp fully the meaning of these tragic events, we need to recall some of Alexander's actions which had, for several years, seriously disturbed the Macedonians.

The first sign of a change in Alexander can be dated to the sojourn in Egypt, when he decided to consult the priests of the famous sanctuary of Amun in the Siwa oasis. According to ancient writers, the difficult journey was marked by miraculous and divine phenomena. The king was received by the priests and taken on his own into the "holy of holies" by the high priest. There are therefore no eyewitnesses to this "interview" between king and god, and all we have are

---

[42] The bibliography here, too, is large, with many debates, which is not surprising given the lack of agreement in the sources. There are in fact so many contradictions that doubt has been cast on the factual reality of this or that episode. Apart from Bosworth, *Conquest and Empire*: 101–104; 114–18, see also, *e.g.*, Badian in B14 (2000): 64–72 (Philotas/Cleitus/Callisthenes) reprinted in B17 (2003): 273–95 and in B22 (2010); as well as B16 (2003): 113–26 (Philotas/Adams), 127–46 (Cleitus/Tritle).

controversial and contradictory accounts that are difficult to disentangle. The one theme common to all is that Alexander declared himself to be the son of Amun. His action and the interpretation of the interview that he himself gave seemingly served several ends. It was, first of all, a gesture towards the cities of Greece, where Sparta was fueling the flames of hatred against Macedon. In Greece Amun was assimilated to Zeus, and his sanctuary at Siwa was particularly famous. The visit was also one of several moves aimed at pleasing the Egyptians. Conversely, nothing proves that Alexander wished, at that date, to be recognized as a god by the Greeks, let alone by the Macedonians, who nonetheless disapproved of this development, their feelings a mixture of irony and ill humor.[43]

All the ancient writers note that from 330 onwards there was an observable change in Alexander's personality, as the king increasingly adopted Persian customs. Obviously the behavior these writers considered proof of "the enervating effects of oriental behavior" is also explicable by the fact that the king needed to win the respect of the Iranian aristocracy. Classical authors were particularly struck by his adoption of Persian ceremonial dress. Even though Alexander only wore it on special occasions, the Macedonians disapproved.[44]

The trial of Philotas,[45] the first incident referred to

[43] Arrian III.3–4; the other sources and discussions are presented in Bosworth, *Commentary* I: 269–75, and "Alexander and Ammon," *Studies Schachermeyr* (1977): 51–75; the episode is endlessly discussed: "We simply cannot tell exactly what happened" (E. Badian, "Alexander between Two Thrones," [1996]: 18 = B17 [2003]: 245–62).

[44] On the negative image of Alexander, see Briant, *Darius dans l'ombre*: 249–84; on the adoption of Achaemenid court etiquette, see the reasoned analysis by Bosworth, "Alexander and the Iranians," *JHS* 100 (1980): 4–8 [B14 (2003): 208–35].

[45] See primarily Arrian III.26; Quintus Curtius VI.7–11; Plutarch, *Alexander* 45–49.

above, came to a head under the following circumstances. Philotas was a leading figure: a son of Parmenion and commander of the cavalry since the start of the expedition. In 330 he was accused in the capital of Drangiana of having fomented a plot to kill the king. The king initiated the affair, with his counsellor Craterus, a personal enemy of Philotas, playing a major role. Alexander then called an assembly of the army and during a dramatic session, Philotas presented a brilliant defense. At the end, the king had him tortured "to force a confession"; the following day, a second assembly condemned Philotas to death (or confirmed the sentence) and proceeded to stone him on the spot.

The whole business remains extremely obscure. But if one reads the ancient accounts dispassionately, the conviction grows very quickly that Philotas was not guilty of the plot of which he stood accused. What is likely is that he, like many other nobles, was opposed to Alexander's adoption of Achaemenid customs. This seems to have constituted a pretext for the king, rather than a genuine reason for his rage against Philotas. This real motivation was probably to eliminate a family that had never been wholehearted in its support for him. This explains why in his speech he related the case of Philotas to that of the pretenders who had emerged at Philip's death.

The timing by which Alexander chose to remove his opponents or bring them to heel is very significant. Up to this point he had tolerated Parmenion's meddling. From 330 on, he no longer felt the same solidarity with "the old Macedonians." He wanted to continue his campaign with those nobles only whose acceptance of his authority was unquestioning, men such as Hephaestion, Craterus, and Perdiccas. Parmenion was executed by a commando sent expressly for this purpose to Media. It was a brutal act, and it showed all too clearly that Alexander would henceforth brook no opposition.[46] Further, calling together the assembly allowed him to unify the army around his person at a point when Macedonian support was becoming ever less reliable.

During a victory banquet held in Maracanda in Sogdiana in the winter of 328/7, a violent quarrel broke out between Alexander and his long-time companion Kleitos, "the Black." Kleitos, as a brother of the royal nurse, was a close friend of the king and always near him in battle. After Philotas's death, he, together with Hephaestion, had assumed command of the cavalry.[47] Alexander's fury was such that he pierced Kleitos with one blow of his spear.[48] It is said that the guests at the banquet were drunk, and that Alexander, horrified by Kleitos's death, was overcome with extreme remorse. But this should not let us lose sight of the central fact of the continued opposition of the Macedonian nobility to a king whose behavior departed increasingly from theirs.

The accusations that Kleitos leveled at Alexander in the course of the banquet show that Philotas's execution and the assassination of Parmenion had driven underground rather than destroyed the opposition of the Macedonian nobles (or of some at least) to the transformation of royal power into autocracy. Kleitos had cited Euripides in order to accuse Alexander of claiming all glory for the Macedonian victories for himself, and of too readily forgetting the parts played by his father Philip and his own generals; the victories had been achieved by all the Macedonians, Kleitos insisted, glory should not redound solely to their leader. Here Kleitos articulated in public what Philotas, according to the

[46] See Badian, "Conspiracies," in B14 (2000): 67–69 (who thinks that the elimination of Parmenion was Alexander's principal concern); cf. Badian's "The death of Parmenio," (1960), reprinted in B22 (2010).

[47] Cf. Heckel, *Marshals of Alexander's Empire* (1992): 34–37.

[48] See Arrian IV.7–9; Quintus Curtius VIII.1.19–52; Plutarch, *Alex.* 50–52.1–2.

classical writers, had expressed in private. Kleitos was also defending the traditional image of Macedonian kingship, which was not personal but contractual and regulated by custom. Alexander was obliged to respect certain usages: he could not govern by simply issuing orders, but had to use persuasion; and in their relations with the king, the Macedonians had an equal right to speak (*isegoria*). Kleitos was clearly accusing Alexander of taking on ever more the trappings of an absolute oriental monarch and turning his back on Macedonian traditions.[49]

Last there was the *proskynesis* affair, which came to a head in the town of Bactra in 327, some time after Alexander's marriage to Roxane. The challenger on this occasion was Callisthenes, Aristotle's nephew, who had shown himself up to this moment to be one of the king's most attentive courtiers.[50] On this occasion, Alexander "ordered that the Macedonians, like the Persians, should greet him prostrated on the ground and offering adoration." According to Quintus Curtius, the king was encouraged to do this by his Greek courtiers. But in fact, as Arrian observes, Alexander had no need of anyone's encouragement to issue this order which, as we shall see, did not have the significance that ancient authors have assigned it.[51] Among the Persians, kneeling or inclining the upper part of the body (*proskynesis*) accompanied by a hand gesture was the regular way of acknowledging a superior; it was not an act of worship. The Persepolis reliefs illustrate this mode of paying homage to the Great King very clearly (Fig. 8). The Greeks were well aware of the meaning of this gesture, which is also depicted on seal im-

[49] See in particular Arrian IV.8.4–6.

[50] See Arrian IV.10–12; Quintus Curtius VIII.5.5–24, 6–7; Plutarch, *Alex.* 52.3–9, 53–55.

[51] Arrian IV.10.5–7, 11–12, with Bosworth, *Commentary* II: 68–90, where the sources and debates are reviewed.

Fig. 8. A royal audience. Relief panel from the Persepolis Treasury, early fifth c. BC, Tehran Museum. Original drawing by Ann Britt Tilia, *Studies and Restorations at Persepolis*, Rome 1972, 190–91. Copyright © Istituto Italiano per l'Africa e l'Oriente (IsIAO).

pressions at Daskyleion, and on the shield of a soldier on the sarcophagus known as the Alexander Sarcophagus.[52]

The Persians were in no sense honoring the king as a divinity. He was never considered to be one; he was only the earthly lieutenant of Auramazda. So for the Persians in Alexander's entourage, this order was nothing remarkable; it was natural for them to offer Alexander the same homage as they had been accustomed to offer to the Great King. But the Greeks and Macedonians (and thus the authors who tell us about the affair) saw things quite differently, as Callisthenes explained. They regarded the gesture as a visible mark of "oriental servility." The Greeks of Asia Minor had

[52] See Briant, *History*: 209–10; Kuhrt, *Persian Empire* II (2007): 534–39; S. Paspalas, *Klio* 87/1 (2005): 72–81. On the *proskynesis* ritual, see *History*, 222–23 and 913–14; on the relationship between the Great King and the gods, *History*, 240–54, 915–17.

been obliged to humiliate themselves by performing the act of *proskynesis* before high Persian officers, and the same obligation when greeting the Great King had created problems of protocol for embassies. With the approval of the Macedonian leaders, Callisthenes refused to perform this form of homage which, he said, should be reserved for the gods. He stressed, just as Kleitos had, that in making this demand Alexander was violating the "unwritten law" (*nomos*) of the Macedonians, according to which the kings should govern "not by force, but in conformity with *nomos*."[53] The king did not forgive Callisthenes. He took advantage of the discovery of an obscure and dangerous affair, the "conspiracy of the pages," to incriminate him. Callisthenes was arrested, held for several years in chains and possibly crucified in India on Alexander's orders. (The tragic fate of Callisthenes gave rise to numerous didactic stories.)

Nowhere is there any suggestion that Alexander was trying to establish his power on a theocratic base. Alexander's goal in 327 was to incorporate as many Iranians as possible into the court and the administration. Many Bactrian and Sogdian nobles had already rallied to his side. But what Alexander wanted was that all his companions, Macedonian and Iranian, should occupy the same position in relation to himself. This explains the organization of the ceremony of offering formal homage to the king in Bactra. The Macedonians' refusal, whether expressed openly or concealed, was not merely a theoretical issue. It showed that they continued to regard the Iranians as beneath them, the vanquished foe, and they were intent on treating them as such. Alexander was sensible enough not to insist on the ceremony, and *proskynesis* was evidently not demanded again from the Macedonians.

[53] Arrian IV.11.16.

The episode bears witness to Alexander's pragmatism. Although by nature authoritarian, the king could admit (to himself if not in public) an error of judgment. Furthermore, from the moment he reached India, it was certainly not in his interest to create the conditions in which a breach with the Macedonian nobility would become inevitable. The affair also shows the extraordinary problems arising from the policy that Alexander was putting to the test: coming from two different cultures, the Iranians and Macedonians responded in contrasting ways to his plans. He may have hoped that the military expedition to India undertaken in common would allow the Iranian and Macedonian nobility to get to know and appreciate each other better.

A Policy for the Future (325–323)

The Return from India

On his return from India, Alexander made plain his resolve to promote the policy of collaboration with the local aristocracy. Several measures expressive of this were aimed at the satraps. The generals in charge of Media—Cleander, Sitalces, and Heracon—were executed because they had helped themselves to the property of the priestly caste and probably to that of the nobility as well.[54] But we should note that the measures taken against the guilty satraps had some paradoxical consequences: by 323 only three Iranian satraps still held that post: Atropates in Media, Phrataphernes in Parthia, and Oxyartes (Alexander's father-in-law) in the Parapamisadae. It is also the case that, in Alexander's absence, some

[54] On Alexander's measures against satraps accused of malpractice and "poor administration," see esp. Arrian VI.27.4–5.

Persian and Iranian leaders had tried to foment revolt—or at least were accused of having done so. This suggests that one section of the Iranian nobility was no longer prepared to support its new master.[55] But the situation must not be exaggerated: these "rebels" did not carry the population with them, and it would be wrong to think that because of these malcontents Alexander abandoned his Iranian policy.

At the same time, Alexander sought to install in the satrapies that had fallen vacant men he thought committed to, and capable of, applying his policy of Macedonian-Iranian collaboration. The best example of this is Peukestas, who had played an important role during the Indian campaign, once even saving the king's life (during the siege of the town of the Mallians, 326/5), for which he was rewarded with a gold crown and the title of *somatophylax* (bodyguard). On his return, Alexander appointed him satrap of the important province of Persis, because Peukestas had adopted the Iranian way of life and so ran no risk of offending the "barbarians." This is how Arrian describes it:

> And of this he gave proof, as soon as he was appointed satrap of Persia, by adopting, alone of the Macedonians, the Median dress and learning the Persian language, and in all other respects assimilating himself to the Persian ways. For this Alexander commended him, and the Persians were gratified that he preferred their ways to those of his own country. (VI.30.2–3)

Alexander saw in this the only way "of keeping the subjugated nation obedient."[56] But it is worthwhile emphasizing, as does Arrian, that Peukestas was an exception and that his behavior aroused the hostility of the other Macedonian

---

[55] See the list in Badian, "Conspiracies," in B14 (2000): 90–95.
[56] Diodorus XIX.14.5.

commanders; even those who were prepared to govern together with the defeated were not prepared to Persianize themselves.

The Weddings at Susa (February 324)

If we keep in mind Alexander's twin concerns of recruiting the Iranian nobility and persuading the Macedonians to accept them, it will help us to understand the significance of the grand ceremony held at Susa early in 324. On this occasion, Alexander (without repudiating Roxane) married two Achaemenid princesses, Darius's daughter Stateira and Parysatis, daughter of Artaxerxes III. Simultaneously, his friend Hephaestion married Drypetis, Stateira's sister, "because Alexander wanted Hephaestion's children to be his own nephews and nieces." Eventually, the king "persuaded" eighty Companions to marry daughters of the Iranian nobility. The marriages were celebrated with unprecedented pomp—the details were described by the head chamberlain, Chares of Mytilene—and in accordance with Persian ritual. Festivities were held in a giant marquee constructed on the model of the Persian *apadana* (audience hall), and each wife was provided with a lavish dowry by Alexander.[57]

This magnificent occasion extended and trumped Alexander's marriage with the Sogdian princess Roxane in 327, and the weddings at Susa reinforced the king's policy of governing together with his former enemies. Several women came from the Achaemenid family, such as Stateira and Drypetis (daughters of the dead ruler) and Parysatis (a daughter of Ochus/Artaxerxes III); others were daughters of nobles who had either resisted Alexander, such as Spitamenes,

---

[57] See esp. Arrian VII.4.4–5, and Bosworth, "Alexander and the Iranians," *JHS* 100 (1980): 8–9 (B12 [1995], B17 [2003]).

whose daughter Apame was married to Seleucus, or who had joined Alexander's side, such as Artabazus and Atropates. The marriages constituted a veritable pact for governing and the inclusion of several members of the now-defunct royal family made possible a harmonious transition between Persian and Macedonian rule. But it certainly did not mean that Alexander was expecting to turn himself into the Great King—that was never his idea.[58]

No ancient text suggests that the Macedonians received this royal initiative with general enthusiasm. In fact Arrian (VII.6.3, 5) says bluntly that a certain number were deeply shocked.

Towards a Macedonian-Iranian Army: The Opis Mutiny

When Alexander was faced at the Hyphasis with the refusal of the Macedonian soldiers to advance further, he realized that he would not be able to achieve his great projects by relying exclusively on the support of his compatriots. And so, in keeping with his goal of uniting Iranians and Macedonians, he determined to create an army that included both elements. The essential measures needed for achieving this were put in place on his return from India.

The first reform took place within the cavalry around the time of the weddings at Susa.[59] The Iranian mounted soldiers, who had fought as auxiliaries in India, were inducted into the *hetairoi* (Companion) cavalry, "that is, those who seemed conspicuous for being handsome or having

[58] I am not persuaded by the scenario imagined by Badian ("Subject and Ruler," reprinted in B22 [2010]: 22–24). His idea that Alexander had planned to have himself invested at Pasargadae, but the magi showed their opposition by sacking the tomb of Cyrus, is pure speculation.

[59] See esp. Arrian VII.6.3–4, and the balanced assessment of Bosworth, "Alexander and the Iranians," *JHS* 100 (1980): 9–10.

some other excellence." Further, a new (fifth) hipparchy was created, made up in large part of Iranians armed with the Macedonian lance rather than the "barbarian" javelin and under the command of the Bactrian noble Hystaspes. Representatives of the flower of the Iranian aristocracy (one of Artabazus's sons, two sons of Mazday/Mazaeus, a brother of Roxane, and more), the very people who became brothers-in-law to Macedonian nobles at the Susa wedding feast, were among his lieutenants. These two measures—matrimonial and military—combined to bring about the fusion of the two aristocracies.

The creation of a mixed phalanx met with considerable resistance. Thirty thousand young Iranians (*epigonoi*: successors) levied in 327 on Alexander's orders arrived in Susa, but they were not formed into a new phalanx until 323, when Peukestas brought a further contingent of twenty thousand Iranians to the king at Babylon.[60] The delay was due to the opposition from the rank and file of Alexander's Macedonian phalanx. The young Iranians formed a totally distinct phalanx for several months, constituted on the model of the Macedonian one but commanded by Persians.

The crisis came to a head in the summer of 324 at Opis on the Tigris, when Alexander announced to the army that the men no longer fit for service (due to wounds or age) would be sent back to Macedon with substantial severance pay. The infantry took this as proof that Alexander no longer wanted their service and would, henceforth, rely exclusively on the Iranian phalanx. Although the Macedonians, as we saw, wished to return home, they wanted to go all

[60] See in particular Arrian VII.23.1–4.

together and with their king. Sending the veterans and the wounded home was seen as a clear indication that the king "was going to set up his kingdom in Asia, which would be the centre of his kingdom."[61] Alexander had the leaders of the mutiny executed and tried to bring the rank and file around by listing the many benefits they owed to Philip II and himself. It did not work.[62]

During the next few days, Alexander made no attempt to reconcile himself with his soldiers. Instead he withdrew to his tent, refused the Macedonians access, and showered the Iranians with favors.[63] He even called an assembly of the Iranian soldiers, in which the Macedonians were forbidden to participate, and he put himself at the head of the Iranian army encamped outside the town as though he were preparing to fight the Macedonian army. He also granted the Iranian infantry soldiers the title of *pezhetairoi* (foot companions), which put them on a level of complete equality with the Macedonians, and enrolled Iranians in the *agema*, the royal bodyguard. By means of these and other measures, Alexander aimed to make the Macedonians believe that he could henceforth dispense with them, and this psychological blackmail had the expected result. After several days, the Macedonian soldiers presented themselves without arms

[61] See chapter III, n. 46.

[62] The famous "mutiny at Opis" is known to all the ancient sources. Many obscurities and uncertainties remain, created in particular by the very literary nature of the ancient reconstructions, especially Alexander's celebrated speech to his troops (Arrian VII.9–10; cf. B. Nagle, "The Cultural Context of Alexander's Speech at Opis," *TAPhA* 126 [1996]: 151–72).

[63] On Alexander's tactics during the mutiny, see the thoughts of E. Carney, "Macedonians and Mutiny: Discipline and Indiscipline in the Army of Philip and Alexander," *Classical Philology* 91 (1996): 19–44; "Artifice and Alexander history," in A. B. Bosworth & E. Baynham, eds., *Alexander the Great in Fact and Fiction*, Oxford (2000): 263–85, esp. 278–85.

before the king, and humbly begged him to permit them—like the Persians!—to bestow on him the ceremonial kiss. Alexander accepted their request and to show his forgiveness called them his "relatives."[64]

Alexander's skill is astounding: he succeeded in getting the Macedonians to accept what only a few days earlier they had obstinately refused. Henceforth, the king had license to do whatever he wished. The departure of the veterans was calm, and the king promised to take care of the children they were leaving behind, and to turn them into soldiers trained and armed in the Macedonian manner. At the same time, he ordered Antipater to send him further Macedonian reinforcements. The new phalanx was formed in Babylon in 323: each of the divisions (decades) of the Macedonian phalanx comprised four Macedonians armed in the Macedonian manner, and twelve Persians equipped with bows and javelins; but the command remained in the hands of Macedonians.

In the space of two years (324–323), Alexander succeeded in mobilizing a completely new army in which Macedonians and Iranians served cheek by jowl. In the short term, this made it possible for him to contemplate his immediate plans for further conquests with renewed optimism, as he was well aware that Macedon was exhausted by his continuous manpower levies.[65] As for his chances for long-term success, the best guarantees would be seeing the territories gathered into a unified empire and Macedonians and Iranians collaborating in a combined army.

[64] See Briant, *Rois, tributs et paysans:* 32–39.
[65] On this point, the debates on how to evaluate the statistics continue, *e.g.,* Bosworth, *The Legacy of Alexander,* Oxford 2002: 64–97: "Macedonian Numbers at the Death of Alexander the Great," where he replies to the critical responses published since the appearance of his article in *JHS* 106 (1986): 1–12.

Fig. 9. Central part of a panel of the "Alexander Sarcophagus," showing Alexander (?) and the Macedonians hunting lions alongside Persian hunters. Late fourth c. BC, Archaeological Museum, Istanbul, Turkey. Photo credit: Erich Lessing / Art Resource, NY.

The Banquet at Opis

Did Alexander want to extend this Macedonian-Iranian collaboration and promote an ideal of "universal brotherhood"? W. W. Tarn believed so, basing his view on the account of the sacrifice performed by the king at the end of the mutiny at Opis:

> Alexander in his gratitude for this, sacrificed to the gods to whom he was wont to sacrifice, and gave a general feast, sitting himself there, and all the Macedonians sitting round him; and then next to them Persians, and next any of the other tribes who had precedence in reputation or any other quality, and he himself and his comrades drank from the

same bowl and poured the same libations, while the Greek seers and the magians began the ceremony. And Alexander prayed for all sorts of blessings, and especially for harmony (*homonoia*) and fellowship (*koinonia*) in the empire between Macedonians and Persians. They say that those who shared the feast were nine thousand, and that they all poured the same libation and thereat sang the song of victory. (Arrian VII.11.8–9)

On the basis of this text, Tarn concluded that Alexander "pioneered one of the greatest revolutions in world history," namely "the brotherhood of man and the unity of mankind." Alexander had wanted to unite all the peoples of the earth in the same spirit of brotherhood; he wanted all peoples to be involved in governing the empire rather than being subjects. Unfortunately, this image of Alexander as a Christlike bringer of peace was more a consequence of Tarn's personal thinking than of a critical reading of the text. As Badian[66] rightly argued, the Opis banquet does not permit such an interpretation. The only people around the king were the Macedonians, who alone shared the king's wine. The chief protagonists in the ceremony of reconciliation were Alexander and the Macedonians, who had just been violently at odds for several days. Moreover there was never any question of universal brotherhood; on the contrary, the collaboration in power was limited expressly to the Macedonians and Persians.

The symbolism of the banquet at Opis illustrates well the two facets of Alexander's policy—on the one hand he made an appeal to the Iranian contingents with the goal of

[66] Both Tarn's and Badian's texts are frequently reprinted: cf. B2 (1966): 243–86 and 287–306, B3 (1974): 77–92, B8 (1992): 73–106, B12 (1995): 210–13 (extracts from Tarn), B17 (2003): 205–7 (Tarn), B22 (2010): Chapter 1 (Badian); on Badian's position, see also his own remarks in B4 (1976): 287–96.

consolidating the conquest, while on the other he reserved for the Macedonians the prime positions around his person. Henceforth, the boundary between rulers and ruled was not to coincide precisely with the boundary between conquerors and conquered. The division would be social rather than ethnic. Only those who had made up the ruling elite of the Achaemenid empire were called upon to take up the reins of government. While this shows that Alexander was able to rise above the traditional Greek notion of a natural opposition between Greeks and Barbarians, it also illustrates his remarkable political intelligence and his desire to ensure the durability of his work.

The Problem of Alexander's Divinization

Given his concern to unify the empire, did Alexander also think of promoting a "cult of empire, extending to the Greek cities of Europe"?[67] This question has been asked for a long time and has provoked diverse answers: "No other object of his career has been so extensively discussed and so hotly debated by modern scholars."[68]

Pictorial representations of Alexander reveal the king's desire to spread an image of himself as an unrivaled superman like the heroes of old, if not the gods themselves. Alexander had, in fact, taken official artists along on his conquests, who were commissioned to do just that: the sculptor Lysippos, the painter Apelles, and the goldsmith Pyrgoteles.

---

[67] On this difficult problem, see the two studies of E. Badian, one in *Ancient Macedonian Studies in Honour of Ch. F. Edson*, Thessaloniki 1981: 27–71, the other in A. Small, ed., *Subject and Ruler*, Ann Arbor, MI 1996: 11–26 = B17 (2003): 245–62.

[68] E. Fredricksmeyer in B15 (2003): 253–78, which provides a synthesis (one of many) and a bibliography (the quote is on p. 253); see also B2 (1966): 151–204, 235–42; B7 (1987) I: 309–34; B12 (1995): 165–202; B17 (2003): 236–72; B22 (2010): two articles by Badian (cf. already B17).

Alexander is frequently shown with his eyes turned heavenward, and Plutarch makes the meaning of this pose clear: Alexander is looking at the heavens as though saying to Zeus, "Take Olympus, leave me the earth!" The artists showed him ever more frequently with his head encircled by a diadem, a royal symbol of eastern origin.[69] The coins, perhaps struck after a model created by Pyrgoteles, clarify the evolution of this iconography. The artist regularly depicted Herakles with a lionskin headdress. But the "Herakles" on the obverse of Alexander's coins is portrayed so individualistically that one is tempted to see here a portrait of Alexander in heroic guise. As these coins circulated throughout the empire, it is easy to imagine that Alexander's assimilation to Herakles was increasingly accepted as a fact, even by the Greek cities.

On the death of Alexander's friend Hephaestion (October 324), Alexander sent an embassy to the oracle of Amun in Egypt, asking whether it would be appropriate to offer divine honors to him. Amun "replied" that Hephaestion should be considered a hero and not a god. Alexander immediately issued orders to Cleomenes in Egypt to erect temples to the new hero in Alexandria and on Pharos.[70] Hephaestion's hero cult spread rapidly and included the Greek cities and Macedon.[71] But there is no clear proof that Athens offered semidivine honors jointly to Hephaestion and Alexander (who would have been regarded as Hephaestion's *paredros*).

[69] See e.g., the discussion by Stewart in B15 (2003): 34–40.

[70] Cf. Arrian VII.23.6–8 (together with Arrian's critical comments).

[71] This is now proved by the dedication on a Macedonian stela (see appendix, n. 37), but nothing indicates that there existed a royal cult in Macedon of Philip and Alexander: cf. M. Mari, "The Ruler Cult in Macedonia," *Studi Ellenistici* XX (2008): 219–68 (232–47).

According to several writers, in 324/3 Alexander wanted his divine character to be officially recognized and took steps to impose his cult throughout the empire. He is said to have ordered Nicanor to proclaim at Olympia in 324, along with the edict ordering the return of exiles, a command that the Greek cities render the king divine honors. This comes from late and rather untrustworthy anecdotes. What we do know is that several cities in Asia Minor honored him with a cult, which was not an exceptional occurrence: Eresos on Lesbos, for example, had raised altars to Philippic Zeus before the Macedonian conquest in 336/5. Evidence from the Greek cities of the European mainland is slight and contradictory. We hear of impassioned debates in Athens between supporters (Demades and, more hesitantly, Demosthenes) and opponents (Lycurgus and Hypereides) of such a move, and of the condemnation of Demades for presenting a decree deemed to be sacrilegious. It is not at all improbable that Alexander had made his wishes known to the leaders in the Greek cities.[72]

In 323 the foundations of Alexander's authority in the various parts of his empire were extremely diverse. He was simultaneously king of the Macedonians, archon of the Thessalian League, *hegemon* of the League of Corinth, Pharaoh in Egypt (whether or not he had been officially recognized as such), and "King of Lands" in Babylonia. By contrast, he certainly never received an Achaemenid royal titulary of any kind. There is just one title, its meaning uncertain and neutral, which all accorded him, that of "King Alexander,"

[72] Cf. Badian in *Subject and Ruler* (1996): 24–26 (reprinted in B17 [2003]: 245–62; cf. 256–58, B22, 2010); Fredricksmeyer in B15 (2003): 274–78.

which we see in simple dating formulas ("Year X of Alexander the King") in various regions and in different languages and scripts, from Lydia to Bactria.

Among all his titles, one retained special importance at all times, even at the most distant points of his conquests and during the fiercest disputes about the adoption of Achaemenid court practices. This was the simple "King of the Macedonians." In that role, Alexander mediated between the gods of his country and the Macedonians.[73] Throughout his expedition, we see him sacrificing to the Macedonian deities.[74] His last days in Babylon are quite typical in this regard, as we know from a kind of record of the king's doings, called the *Ephemerides* by the ancient writers who cite the document (either directly or indirectly). We can see it, for example, in Arrian, where the same expression recurs, day after day:

> He was carried forth on a litter each day to his religious duties and he sacrificed after the usual custom (*pros ta hiera thusai o nomos . . . kai ta hiera epithenta*). . . . Next day, he bathed again and sacrificed the usual sacrifices. . . . Next day . . . he sacrificed the appointed sacrifices. . . . Next day he just contrived to be carried out for the usual sacrifices and offered them. . . . Next day also, being now quite ill, he yet offered the usual sacrifices. (VII.25)

It is important to recognize that Alexander never forgot his sacred obligation, that even during his last days he continued to fulfill his most fundamental duty as "King of the Macedonians."

[73] Cf. Briant, *Antigone le Borgne*: 323 with the long footnote 2.
[74] The sources are collected in Berve, *Alexanderreich* I (1925): 85–93.

Conclusion

The King Is Dead! Long Live the King?

Drawing up a balance sheet of Alexander's achievements as of June 323 is difficult, perhaps even impossible. We can see that a substantial number of problems were beginning to arise at the very moment when the Arabian expedition was about to get under way. There were, for example, disturbances within the Greek cities, and there was resistance to his project of reaching an entente with the elites of the former empire of his defeated and assassinated adversary. Should we perhaps conclude that Alexander's conquests had reached a historical impasse?

This is one of the current historiographical trends, and is on the way to becoming the dominant one. It has become rather fashionable to condemn Alexander's conquests out of hand, both for political and "moral" reasons: Alexander was a "butcher of people," perhaps no more than a "terrorist," or just a "hooligan." His reign would have been a veritable fiasco. He would have been preoccupied with short-term strategies and distracted from the business of government by his marked taste for violence:

> His military aggression, his violent reaction against any demonstration of resistance, the ruthless killing of local populations and the destruction of cities and towns throughout his twelve-year campaign certainly allow such a conclusion.[1]

[1] Quotation from Brosius in B15 (2003): 172, referring to Sancisi-Weerdenburg's conclusion in B9 (1993): 177–88.

139

Alexander was merely a conqueror who did not seek to be seen as a ruler. . . . As a conqueror Alexander failed to maintain an empire and control it for any length of time. . . . The Achaemenid ideology of the *"Pax Persica,"* so embedded in Achaemenid kingship, proved incompatible with the military conquest of Alexander and the imposition of Macedonian power on the Persians.[2]

Another writer, who has also roundly denounced Alexander's bloody brutality and strategic blunders,[3] similarly stresses the king's incapacity to administer the empire and create peace within it.[4] As one critic has observed, while it is certainly right to reject the idea of Alexander as a proponent of "universal brotherhood" expressed in his time by W. W. Tarn, we are now seeing the spread "of a new extreme orthodoxy" that takes a diametrically opposite view of Alexander.[5]

I shall not dwell long on the "moral" judgments that have been passed on Alexander, the inspiration and formulation of which seem to me utterly inappropriate in the context of historical research.[6] An Alexander historian may well harbor a personal hostility to "great conquerors," but his duty nevertheless is to analyze coolly the expectations and consequences of his conquests. The Persian elites were neither more nor less inclined towards peace or war than the Macedonian elites, and the so-called *Pax Persica* was an ideological construction that transformed reality by transfiguring it through the vision of those who held

[2] Brosius B15 (2003): 193.
[3] Worthington *AHB* 11 (1997) = B15 (2003): 303–18.
[4] Worthington, *Alexander the Great*, London (2004): 206–17, where the author picks up the substance of the article cited in the preceding footnote without taking note of the criticisms that have been expressed against the theses he put forward.
[5] Holt, *AHB* 11 (1997) = B15 (2003): 324.
[6] See Briant, *Studi Ellenistici* XVI (2005): 49ff.

power.[7] From Darius to Alexander, we do not move from peaceful harmony to a situation of unbridled violence, or from a wonderfully unified kingship to a destructive reign by Macedonian mafia ruffians, whose only law is that of the jungle.

The thesis of Alexander's failure is obviously arrived at on the basis of events that occurred *after* his death, which led to the break-up of the territories he had conquered and thus to the disappearance of the empire that Cyrus and his successors had built. But is this failure attributable to Alexander or to his successors? Had that history already been written at the beginning of June 323? This appears to be the view of one author, who wrote recently:

> His arrogance was largely responsible for his own early death; and he was also responsible for the ultimate failure of his imperial enterprise. . . . He needed an adult successor, and he both refused to provide one, and killed off any man who could be seen as one.[8]

The sentiments expressed here are a little strange to say the least. Alexander is held responsible not only for the acts and policies of his successors, but also for his own death? I prefer to return to Bishop Bossuet's thoughts—banal though they may be—about Alexander in 1681: "We must not blame his faults, big as they were, for the collapse of his family, but simply human mortality!"

It is true that in the early morning of June 11, 323, Alexander's achievements remained vulnerable, but no one is in a position to say that he would not have been able to build up his empire and consolidate it—unless it is accepted

[7] See in particular the analysis of M. Root, *The King and Kingship in Achaemenid Art*, Leiden 1979; cf. also Briant, *History*: 172–83, 908–11.

[8] J. D. Grainger, *Alexander the Great Failure: The Collapse of the Macedonian Empire*, London 2007, xviii.

141

that his manner of government was inherently malevolent and catastrophic, and that he would therefore have failed to build an empire no matter how long his reign lasted. If that is the case, there is nothing further to discuss.

Let us take, as just one example, the edict concerning the return of the exiles.[9] This can be interpreted in a variety of ways. Should we conclude that Alexander was acting irresponsibly, that he himself helped to plunge Greece into the anti-Macedonian revolt? Or, on the contrary, was he perhaps acting like a clearsighted statesman? While the edict provoked opposition in Athens (because of its "great power" interests in Samos), many Greeks had expected such a measure. Moreover, it was intended to remedy a situation that the cities themselves were incapable of resolving.[10]

Should we also accuse Alexander, as is now commonly done, of not having prepared for the succession?[11] This is the conclusion usually drawn from an anecdote that Diodorus places at the start of the army's departure for the Hellespont. The setting is a war council:

> Antipater and Parmenion advised him to produce an heir first and then to turn his hand to so ambitious an enterprise, but Alexander was eager for action and opposed any postponements and spoke against them. (XVII.16.2)

The story may well have been fabricated after the event, and can be interpreted in various ways. Either Alexander was totally self-centered, more concerned with his own glory than with the future of the dynasty. Or, with an eye on Macedon's history, Alexander decided wisely to avoid favor-

[9] See chapter IV.

[10] See the balanced discussion by Flower in B14 (2000): 126–28, and by Farraguna in B15 (2003): 124–30; also Hammond and Walbank (1988) in B17 (2003): 85–86.

[11] Apart from Grainger, n. 8 above, see Worthington, n. 4 above: 211.

ing one noble clan over another.[12] However that may be, the fact remains that Alexander had a son with Artabazus's daughter Barsine, and a little later married Roxane; at the beginning of June 323, his Iranian wife was pregnant.[13] This makes it hard to accuse Alexander of ignoring the future of his lineage. We should also note that if he had married just before leaving, his son (on the assumption that he had a son rather than two girls!) would have been ten years old when Alexander died. To judge by the behavior of the Successors with respect to the Argead lineage, it is not at all certain that the young man would have stood much chance!

Moreover, Alexander in fact did have an heir, namely Arrhidaeus, his half-brother, who was proclaimed king by the rank and file with the name Philip. A few months later, Alexander's posthumously born son by Roxane (named Alexander) was associated with Arrhidaeus as king. In 323, Arrhidaeus was roughly the same age as Alexander—or perhaps one or two years older. Little is known of his life and personality. We do not know whether he had accompanied his brother already in 334, or had joined Alexander only shortly before 323. He is supposed to have suffered from mental and psychological backwardness, but Quintus Curtius does not present the same picture. Even if we grant the fact that he did not have a strong personality, nothing prevented him from being made king.[14]

Quintus Curtius says that when the rank and file picked

---

[12] See E. Baynham, "Why Didn't Alexander Marry Before Leaving Macedonia? Observations on Factional Policies at Alexander's Court in 336–334 B.C.," *Rheinisches Museum* 141 (1998): 141–52; see also the apt observations of E. Carney, *Women and Monarchy in Macedonia* (2000): 97–100.

[13] See Carney, 100–17.

[14] On Arrhidaeus's character, see W. S. Greenwalt, "The Search for Arrhidaeus," *Ancient World* 10 (1984): 69–77, and now, above all, the very well-researched and welcome study of E. Carney, "The Trouble with Philip Arrhidaeus," *AHB* 15/2 (2001): 63–89, which reevaluates Quintus Curtius's evidence on his character.

Alexander's successor, it was because "he [was] the son of Philip, brother of Alexander, who was shortly before king, (and) recently (*paulo ante*) [the king's] associate in sacrifices and ceremony (*sacrorum caerimoniarumque consors modo*)."[15] This was the qualification that in the eyes of ordinary Macedonians made him Alexander's most suitable heir. And as we have seen the importance Alexander accorded to his religious duties as Macedonian king, the information further suggests that shortly before his death (*paulo ante*), it was none other than Alexander who had "associated" his brother with himself.[16] The end of the story was no longer his responsibility.

[15] Quintus Curtius X.7.2. I have already explained briefly elsewhere (Briant, *History*: 1050) why I cannot accept the Babylonian interpretation of the episode by Bosworth (*Chiron* 1992); see now T. Boiy (in Briant and Joannès, eds., *La Transition*: 70–71), who comes to the same conclusion independently.

[16] On the distinction between religious functions and political and military functions, see Briant, *Antigone*: 323–26. Obviously, this is only a hypothesis: but at least it has the merit, in my view, of being based on a credible text, and not on the improbable assumption that Alexander was irresponsible.

An Introductory Bibliography

The bibliography given here is selective. The footnotes in the text provide additional references, which can be used to compile thematic bibliographies. For completeness, use the bibliographical compilation in the appendix.

INTERNET SITES

On Alexander, see in particular http://people.clemson.edu/~elizab/alexhome.htm (ed. E. Carney). For the Persian empire, see http://www.achemenet.com and http://www.achemenet-museum.college-de-france.fr (both ed. P. Briant).

LITERARY SOURCES: TEXTS AND COMMENTARIES

Arrian

Arrian, *Anabasis Alexandrou and Indica*, trans. P. A. Brunt, Loeb Classical Library I–II, 1976–83.

A. B. Bosworth, *A Historical Commentary on Arrian's History of Alexander* I–II, Oxford 1980, 1995.

————, *From Arrian to Alexander*, Oxford 1988.

P. A. Stadter, *Arrian of Nicomedia*, Chapel Hill, NC 1980.

H. Tonnet, *Recherches sur Arrien. Sa personnalité et ses écrits atticistes* I–II, Amsterdam 1988.

P. Vidal-Naquet, "Flavius Arrien entre deux mondes," in Arrien, *Histoire d'Alexandre* (French trans. P. Savinel), Paris 1984, 311–94.

Justin

J. C. Yardley and W. Heckel, *Justin, Epitome, Books 11–12: Alexander the Great*, Oxford 1997.

L. Braccesi et al., *L'Alessandro di Giustino*, Rome 1993.

Diodorus Siculus

Diodorus Siculus, *Library of History*, Book XVII, trans. C. B. Welles, Loeb Classical Library VIII, 1963.

Diodorus Siculus, *Bibliothèque historique, livre* XVII (French trans. P. Gou-kowsky), Paris 1976.

Plutarch

Plutarch, *Alexander,* trans. B. Perrin, Loeb Classical Library VII, 1914.

J. R. Hamilton, *Plutarch, Alexander. A Commentary,* Oxford 1969.

Quintus Curtius

Quintus Curtius, *History of Alexander* I–II, trans. J. C. Rolfe, Loeb Classical Library, 1971.

J. E. Atkinson, *A Commentary on Q. Curtius Rufus' Historiae Alexandri Magni, Books 3 and 4,* Amsterdam 1980; *Books 5 to 7.2,* Amsterdam 1994.

J. E. Atkinson and J. C. Yardley, *Curtius Rufus, Histories of Alexander the Great, Book 10,* Oxford 2009.

E. Baynham, *Alexander the Great: The Unique History of Quintus Curtius,* Ann Arbor, MI 1998.

Aelian

Aelian, *Historical Miscellany,* trans. N. G. Wilson, Loeb Classical Library, 1997.

L. Prandi, "L'Alessandro di Eliano," in *Memorie storiche dei Greci in Claudio Eliano,* Rome 2005, 81–90.

Fragments

F. Jacoby, *Die Fragmente der griechischen Historiker* IIB, Leiden 1926, 618–828 (Greek text only) and *Die Fragmente IIB (Kommentar),* Leiden 1962, 403–542. For translations and new commentaries, see *Brill's New Jacoby,* ed. I. Worthington, Leiden (electronic resource: http://www.brill.nl/brillsnewjacoby [by subscription]).

J. Auberger, *Historiens d'Alexandre,* Paris 2001 (Greek text and French translation).

L. Pearson, *The Lost Histories of Alexander the Great,* New York and London 1960.

P. Pédech, *Historiens compagnons d'Alexandre,* Paris 1984.

C. A. Robinson, *The History of Alexander the Great I: A Translation of the Extant Fragments,* Providence, RI 1953 (English translation only).

BIBLIOGRAPHY

Epigraphic, Numismatic, and Iconographic Sources

Epigraphic Documents from Asia Minor

Alexander's dedication at the Létôon of Xanthos: *Bulletin Épigraphique* 1980, nr. 487.

A. Bencivenni, *Progetti di reforme constituzionali nelle epigrafi greche dei secoli IV–II a.c.*, Bologna 2003, 15–103.

A. J. Heisserer, *Alexander the Great and the Greeks: The Epigraphical Evidence*, Norman, OK 1980.

Macedonian Inscriptions

R. M. Errington, "Neue epigraphische Belege für Makedonien zur Zeit Alexanders des Grossen," in B13 (1998): 77–90.

M. Hatzopoulos, *Macedonian Institutions under the Kings* II, Athens and Paris 1996.

———, "Alexandre en Perse. La revanche et l'empire," *ZPE* 116 (1997): 41–52.

———, "Macédoine," in the *Bulletin épigraphique* of *REG* (from 1987 onwards).

Numismatic Sources

F. L. Holt, *Alexander the Great and the Mystery of the Elephant Medallions*, Berkeley, CA 2003.

G. Le Rider, *Alexander the Great: Coinage, Finances and Policy* (English trans.), Philadelphia, PA 2007.

M. Price, *The Coinage in the Name of Alexander the Great and Philip Arrhidaeus* I–II, London 1991.

F. Smith, *L'immagine di Alessandro il Grande sulle monete del regno (336–323 a.C.)*, Milan 2000.

Iconographic Sources

P. Briant, *Darius dans l'ombre d'Alexandre*, Paris 2003, 226–47, 501–13.

Catalogue of the exhibition "*Alessandro Magno. Storia e mito*," Rome (Fondazione Memmo) 1995.

Catalogue of the exhibition "*Alexander der Grosse und die Öffnung der Welt*," S. Hansen, A. Wieczorek, and M. Tellenbach, eds., Mannheim 2009.

A. Cohen, *The Alexander Mosaic*, Cambridge 1997.

W. Heckel, "Mazaeus, Callisthenes and the Alexander Sarcophagus," *Historia* 55 (2006): 385–96.

M. Pfrommer, *Untersuchungen zur Chronologie und Komposition des Alexandermosaiks*, Mainz 1998.

A. Stewart, *Faces of Power. Alexander's Image and Hellenistic Politics*, Berkeley, CA 1993.

SOURCES FROM THE ACHAEMENID REGIONS

Lydian Inscriptions

T. Boiy, "Alexander Dates in Lydian Inscriptions," *Kadmos* 44 (2005): 165–74.

Egyptian Sources

M. Abd El-Raziq, *Die Darstellung und Texte des Sanktuars Alexanders des Grossen im Tempel von Luxor*, Mainz am Rhein 1984.

M. Chauveau and C. Thiers, "L'Égypte en transition," in eds. P. Briant and F. Joannès, *La transition entre l'empire achéménide et les royaumes hellénistiques* (*Persika* 9), Paris 2006, 375–404 (390–92, 397–99).

D. Schäfer, "Alexander der Grosse—Pharao und Priester," in ed. S. Pfeiffer, *Ägypten unter fremden Herrschern zwischen persischer Satrapie und römischer Provinz*, Frankfurt-am-Main 2007, 54–74.

Aramaic Documents from Syria-Transeuphrates

P. Briant, "The Empire of Darius in Perspective," in B20 (2009): 146, 152–55 (with bibliography).

A. Lemaire, in eds. P. Briant and F. Joannès, *La transition entre l'empire achéménide et les royaumes hellénistiques* (*Persika* 9), Paris 2006, 405–42.

Babylonian Cuneiform Tablets

P. Bernard, "Nouvelle contribution de l'épigraphie cunéiforme à l'histoire hellénistique," *BCH* 114 (1990): 513–28 (515–28).

P. Briant and F. Joannès, eds., *La transition entre l'empire achéménide et les royaumes hellénistiques* (*Persika* 9), Paris 2006, 17–36 (P.-A. Beaulieu), 37–100 (T. Boiy), 101–35 (F. Joannès), 137–222 (M. Jursa), 223–60 (M. W. Stolper), 261–307 (R. Van der Spek).

A. Kuhrt, "Alexander and Babylon," *AchHist* V (1991): 121–30.

———, *The Persian Empire: A Corpus of Sources from the Achaemenid Period* I, London 2007, 447–48.

———, "Survey of Written Sources Available for the History of Babylonia under the Later Achaemenids (concentrating on the period from Artaxerxes II to Darius III)," *AchHist* I (1987): 147–57.

BIBLIOGRAPHY

A. J. Sachs and H. Hunger, *Astronomical Diaries and Related Texts from Babylonia* I, Vienna 1988, 165–219.

M. W. Stolper, "On Some Aspects of Continuity between Achaemenid and Hellenistic Babylonian Texts," *AchHist* VIII (1994): 329–54.

R. Van der Spek, "Darius III, Alexander the Great and Babylonian Scholarship," *AchHist* XIII (2003): 289–346.

See also http://www.livius.org/cg-cm/chronicles/chron00.html (Babylonian chronicles: pre-publication by I. Finkel and R. Van der Spek).

Aramaic Texts from Bactria

P. Briant, "The Empire of Darius in Perspective," in B20 (2009): 148–52.

J. Naveh and S. Shaked, *Aramaic Documents from Bactria (Fourth Century B.C.)*, Corpus Inscriptionum Iranicarum 1.V, London (forthcoming).

S. Shaked, "De Khulmi à Nikhšapaya : les données des nouveaux documents araméens de Bactres sur la toponymie de la région (IVe siècle av. notre ère)," *CRAI* novembre-décembre 2003: 1517–35.

————, *Le satrape de Bactriane et son gouverneur (Persika 4)*, Paris 2003.

Syntheses, Monographs, and Research Tools

H. Berve, *Das Alexanderreich auf prosopographischer Grundlage* I–II, Munich 1926.

E. Borza, *In the Shadow of Olympus: The Emergence of Macedon*, Princeton, NJ 1990.

A. B. Bosworth, *Conquest and Empire: The Reign of Alexander the Great*, Oxford 1988.

————, *Alexander and the East: The Tragedy of Triumph*, Oxford 1996.

P. Briant, *Alexander the Great, Man of Action, Man of Spirit*, New York 1996.

————, *Lettre ouverte à Alexandre le Grand*, Arles 2008.

W. Heckel, *The Marshalls of Alexander's Empire*, London and New York 1992.

————, *Who's Who in the Age of Alexander the Great*, Oxford 2006.

W. Heckel and J. C Yardley, *Alexander the Great: Historical Sources in Translation*, Oxford 2003.

H.-U. Wiemer, *Alexander der Große*, (C. H. Beck Studium) Munich 2005.

The Persian Foe

L. Allen, *The Persian Empire: A History*, London 2005.

P. Briant, *Bulletin d'Histoire Achéménide* [BHAch II], Paris 2001.

P. Briant, *Darius, les Perses et l'empire*, (Coll. Découvertes, Gallimard), Paris (2nd ed.) 2001.

———, *Darius dans l'ombre d'Alexandre*, Paris 2003.

———, "The Empire of Darius in perspective," in W. Heckel and L. Tritle, eds., *Alexander the Great: A New History*, Oxford 2009: 141–70.

———, *From Cyrus to Alexander: History of the Persian Empire* (English translation of *Histoire de l'empire perse: de Cyrus à Alexandre*, Paris 1996), Winona Lake, IN 2002.

———, "New Trends in Achaemenid History," *AHB* 17/1–2 (2003): 33–47.

A. Kuhrt, *The Persian Empire: A Corpus of Sources from the Achaemenid Period* I–II, London 2007.

J. Wiesehöfer, *Ancient Persia* (English translation), London and New York 2001.

HISTORIOGRAPHY AND DEBATES: SOME LANDMARKS

R. Bichler, "Wie lange wollen noch mit Alexander dem Grossen siegen? Karl Christ zum Gedanken," in eds. V. Losemann et al., *Alte Geschichte zwischen Wissenschaft und Politik. Gedenkschrift Karl Christ*, Wiesbaden, 2009, 25–62.

E. N. Borza, "Introduction to Alexander Studies," in U. Wilcken, *Alexander the Great*, New York 1967, ix–xxviii.

A. B. Bosworth, "Alexander the Great and the Creation of the Hellenistic Age," in ed. G. Bugh, *The Cambridge Companion to the Hellenistic World*, Cambridge 2006, 9–26.

———, "The Impossible Dream: W. W. Tarn's *Alexander* in Retrospect," in *Ancient Society: Resources for Teachers* (Macquarie University), XIII/3 (1983): 131–50.

———, "*Ingenium und Macht*. Fritz Schachermeyr and Alexander the Great," *AJAH* 13/1 (1988) [1996]: 56–78.

———, "Johann Gustav Droysen, Alexander the Great and the Creation of the Hellenistic Age," in P. Wheatley and R. Hannah, eds., *Alexander and His Successors: Essays from the Antipodes*, Claremont, CA 2009: 1–27.

B. Bravo, *Philologie, histoire, philosophie de l'histoire. Étude sur J.-G. Droysen historien de l'Antiquité*, Wroclaw-Warsaw-Cracow 1968.

P. Briant, "Alexander the Great," in eds. G. Boy-Stones, B. Graziosi, and P. Vasunia, *The Oxford Handbook of Hellenic Studies*, Oxford 2009, 77–85.

———, "'Alexandre et l'hellénisation de l'Asie': l'histoire au passé et au présent," *Studi Ellenistici* XVI (2003): 9–69.

———, "Alexander and the Persian Empire, between 'Decline' and 'Renovation': History and Historiography," in eds. W. Heckel and L. Tritle, *Alexander the Great: A New History*, Oxford 2009: 171–88.

———, "Michel Rostovtzeff et le passage du monde achéménide au monde hellénistique," *Studi Ellenistici* XX (2008): 137–154.

———, "Montesquieu, Mably et Alexandre le Grand : aux sources de l'histoire hellénistique," *Revue Montesquieu* 8 (2005–2006): 151–85.

K. N. Demetriou, "Historians on Macedonian Imperialism and Alexander the Great," *Journal of Modern Greek Studies* 19 (2001): 23–60.

R. Lane Fox, "Alexander the Great: 'Last of the Achaemenids?,'" in ed. C. Tuplin, *Persian Responses: Political and Cultural Interaction with(in) the Achaemenid Empire*, Swansea 2007, 267–311.

H.-U. Wiemer, "Alexander—der letze Achämenide? Eroberungspolitik, lokale Eliten und altorientalische Traditionen im Jahre 323," *Historische Zeischrift* 284 (2007): 281–309.

Appendix

❧❧❧

The History of Alexander Today: A Provisional Assessment and Some Future Directions

The appendix added here to the American edition is not intended to provide a detailed assessment of the current state of affairs. What I should prefer to do is to explain in what respects and how, at the beginning of the twenty-first century, the history of Alexander appears strangely unchanged, and why, at the same time, it is in a process of transformation. On the occasion of his Inaugural Lecture at University College London in 1952, Arnaldo Momigliano observed, ". . . all students of Ancient History know in their heart that Greek history is passing through a crisis."[1] Almost sixty years later, I am tempted to think that the history of Alexander is passing through a similar phase, namely a "crisis," which can and should be seen positively, provided it is analysed in this way by researchers, teachers, and scholars.

❧❧❧

Even now, the person of Alexander and his history attract attention well beyond the circle of professional ancient historians. Frequently in books on European expansion and colonization, Alexander is seen as a predecessor, and his conquests sometimes serve as an introductory chapter.[2] An-

[1] *George Grote and the Study of Greek History*, London, 1952: 4 (= A.D. Momigliano, *Studies on Modern Scholarship*, Berkeley, CA 1994: 16).

[2] E.g. A. Pagden, *People and Empires: Europeans and the Rest of the World from Antiquity to the Present*, London 2001. In chapter 1, Pagden calls Alexander "the

153

other example arises from the wars conducted by the Americans in Iraq and Afghanistan, which have provoked reflections on "continuities between Alexander and Bush," that are based on an epistemological model whose relevance should categorically be challenged.[3] Some have interested themselves in the history of Alexander as "a fascinating journey into the history of leadership," illustrative of the popular saying: "There is nothing impossible for those who persevere."[4] In a completely different arena, a team of biologists has tried to demonstrate recently that analyses of blood types support the thesis of Macedonian settlement in a valley in the Hindu Kush—a kind of revival of "The Man Who Would Be King"![5]

A spate of specialist books and studies shows clearly how the publicity and release of Oliver Stone's film *Alexander* (2004/2005) stimulated the imagination of publishers and authors. However, the production of these works is in step with the rhythm of a long-established historiographical tradition. It is clearly out of the question to attempt to list them here. The list would be interminable and of little practical value. I will content myself with drawing up two tables, one

first world conqueror" (pp. 13–27), unfortunately forgetting that before him "the most extensive empire the ancient world had ever seen" was in fact the Achaemenid empire.

[3] See F. L. Holt, *Into the Land of Bones: Alexander the Great in Afghanistan*, Berkeley, CA 2005. An excellent specialist on Alexander and Central Asia, Holt states that he is aware of the risk of "presentism," which he nevertheless does not, in my view, avoid; see the apt criticisms of E. Borza (B19 [2007]: 439–40) of a comparable approach taken by J. Romm, "From Babylon to Baghdad: Teaching a Course after 9/11," (B19 [2007]: 431–35).

[4] M.F.R. Kets de Vries and E. Engellau, *Are Leaders Born or Are They Made? The Case of Alexander the Great*, London and New York 2004. The point of the book is indicated by the title of the last chapter: "Leadership Lessons from Alexander the Great."

[5] S. Firasat et al., "Y-chromosomal Evidence for a Limited Greek Contribution to the Pathan Population of Pakistan," *European Journal of Human Genetics* 15 (2007): 121–26. (I owe this reference to my friends, Biaggio Virgilio and Omar Coloru, in Pisa.)

of bibliographical assessments dating to the years 1939 to 1993 (table 1),[6] and the other of collections of articles published between 1965 and 2010 (table 2). Neither table pretends to completeness.

Various critical assessments have appeared in different languages from time to time. The first, edited by H. Bengtson and published in 1939 (A1), analyzed a selection of studies and articles that had appeared since 1933; the last, edited by J. Carlsen (A16), covers the 1970s and 1980s. Those who want, understandably, to go back before 1933, should note that the centenary of the publication of Droysen's work (1833) brought the publication of several monographs (in 1931, Wilcken in German and Radet in French; in 1933, Andreotti in Italian and Tarn in English).

It is also worth consulting the methodological introduction (in Italian) to the monograph by R. Andreotti,[7] which has had a lasting influence (cf. A2, 4, 7), and (in French) the very detailed reviews of P. Roussel and G. Radet of studies published in their time (between 1931 and 1934).[8] Other articles allow for a specific focus, sometimes in a political context.[9] Note also the reissues with commentary of the books by the "great ancestors" (Wilcken,[10] Droysen[11]).

---

[6] The reader will find here global analyses (A1–2, 5, 7–8, 11, 13, 16) and assessments of more specific topics (A3–4, 6, 12, 14–15); there are also two books of a very different sort (A8 and 11).

[7] Il problema politico di Alessandro Magno, Rome 1933: 5–13.

[8] E.g., Journal des Savants, February 1932: 49–60 (Roussel on Wilcken 1931 and Radet 1931); Revue Historique 173 (1934): 80–90 (Radet on Wilcken); Journal des Savants, July–August 1935 (Radet on Tarn 1933, Andreotti 1933, and Bickermann 1934).

[9] E.g., J.-R. Knipfing, "German Historians and Macedonian Imperialism," AHR 26 (1921): 657–71.

[10] The English translation of 1932 was republished in 1967 (New York and London), with "An Introduction to Alexander Studies," by E. N. Borza (pp. ix–xxviii).

[11] The French translation (1883) of the Geschichte des Hellenismus (1877) was republished in 2003 (Ed. Laffont, Paris, 1 vol.) and in 2005 (Ed. J. Millon, Grenoble, 2 vols., with a long introduction by P. Payen, pp. 5–82); the French translation

Since 1990, no one has really taken up the torch. The reason for this might appear to be the sheer magnitude of the task and the discouraging effect of the many difficulties that beset it. Sadly, this is not the case, as the production of works on Alexander has grown to such proportions that it has become an unstoppable flood, with each annual inundation threatening to swamp the sediment deposited by the preceding year's tide! Apart from the innumerable biographies, which, when compared with one another, are all of doubtful originality, many books and manuals devoted to the Hellenistic period include an introductory chapter on the Macedonian conquest.[12] The publications of collected articles (B1–3, 8, 12, 15, 17, 20),[13] and proceedings of specialized colloquia (B4–5, 9, 13–14, 16, 18–19, 23) are beyond number.[14] If we add the volumes of collected essays and articles (B6, 7, 11, 22), we end up with an impressive list of works (table 2) to add to the first one.

The tables call for a few brief comments:

(i) Linked to Europe's cultural history is the decline, amounting to a virtual disappearance, of published scholarship in languages other than English. This is particularly the case for collective works and conference proceedings (B8–23 dating from 1999 to 2009, with the partial exception of B13 [1998]). English-speaking students run the risk of think-

---

(1935) of Droysen 1833 is regularly reissued. For reasons that I do not understand (the instant and firm disagreement expressed by George Grote against Droysen's thesis?), Droysen's books have never been translated into English.

[12] E.g., F. W. Walbank, *The Hellenistic World*, London (1981), chapter 1, "Alexander the Great."

[13] I have not taken into account collections that are not exclusively concerned with Alexander (e.g., Briant, *Rois, tributs et paysans*: 161–74; 281–330; 357–404), nor the issues of *Ancient World* devoted to him in the 1980s and 1990s, nor the series *Ancient Macedonia* (Thessaloniki 1974–).

[14] Cf. http://people.clemson.edu/~elizab/Alexander%20conference.html.

TABLE 1
Critical Bibliographies (1939–93)

A	Date	Author	Title	Reference
1	1939	H. Bengtson	"Alexander und der Hellenismus. Ein Forschungsbericht über Neuerscheinungen"	*Die Welt als Geschichte* 5: 168–87
2	1950	R. Andreotti	"Il problema di Alessandro Magno nella storiografia dell'ultimo decennio"	*Historia* 1: 583–600
3	1954	F. Hampl	"Alexander der Grosse und die Beurteilung geschichtlicher Persönlichkeit in der modernen Historiographie"	*La nouvelle Clio* 6 : 91–136
4	1956	R. Andreotti	"Per una critica dell'ideologia di Alessandro Magno"	*Historia* 5: 256–302
5	1956	A. Gitti	"L'unitarietà della tradizione su Alessandro Magno nella ricerca moderna"	*Athenaeum* 34: 39–57
6	1956	G. Walser	"Zur neueren Forschung über Alexander den Großen"	*Schweizer Beiträge zur Allgemeinen Geschichte* 14: 156–89 (= B2. XVI)
7	1957	R. Andreotti	"Die Weltmonarchie Alexanders des Großen in Überlieferung und geschichtlicher Wirklichkeit"	*Saeculum* 8: 120–66
8	1970	N. Burich	*Alexander the Great: A Bibliography*	The Kent State University Press
9	1971	E. Badian	"Alexander the Great, 1948–67"	*Classical World* 65/2: 37–83
10	1972	A. Demandt	"Politische Aspekte im Alexanderbild der Neuzeit"	*Archiv für Kulturgeschichte* 54: 325–63
11	1972	J. Seibert	*Alexander der Große*	*Erträge der Forschung* 10, Darmstadt
12	1976	E. Badian	"Some Recent Interpretations of Alexander"	*Alexandre le Grand*, Fondation Hardt, Geneva: 279–311
13	1978	A. Jähne	"Alexander der Große. Persönlichkeit, Politik, Ökonomie"	*Jahrbuch für Wirtschaftsgeschichte* 1978/1: 245–63
14	1983	P. Goukowsky	"Recherches récentes sur Alexandre le Grand (1978–82)"	*Revue des Études Grecques* 96: 225–34
15	1986	W. Rubinsohn	"Some remarks on Soviet Historiography of Ancient Macedonia and Alexander the Great"	*Ancient Macedonia* 4: 525–40
16	1993	J. Carlsen	"Alexander the Great (1970–90)"	*Alexander the Great. Myth and reality*, Rome, 41–52

157

TABLE 2
Collected Essays and Anthologies on Alexander (1965–2009)

B	Title	Date	Publisher	Author(s)	Language	Papers
1	Alexander the Great	1965	Greece and Rome XII/1	J. V. Muir, ed.	English	9
2	Alexander the Great: The Main Problems	1966	Cambridge: Heffer	G. T. Griffith, ed.	English (11) German (5)	16
3	The Impact of Alexander the Great	1974	Hinsdale, IL: Dryden Press	E. N. Borza, ed.	English	19
4	Alexandre le Grand. Images et réalités	1976	Geneva: Hardt Foundation	Various	English (5) German (2)	7
5	Alessandro Magno. Tra Storia e mito	1984	Milan: Jaca Books	M. Sordi, ed.	Italian	16
6	Studien z. Alexander-geschichte	1985	Darmstadt: Wiss. Buchgesellschaft, Darmstadt	G. Wirth	German	16
7	Zu Alexander dem Grossen	1987 I–II	Amsterdam: Hakkert	W. Will, ed.	German (39) English (8) French (3) Italian (2)	52
8	Alexander the Great: An Exercise in the Study of History	1992	Melberta, NE: High Butte Books	K. Leyton-Brown, ed.	English	20
9	Alexander the Great: Reality and Myth	1993	Rome: L'Erma	J. Carlsen et al., eds.	English (12) Italian (2) German (1) French (1)	16
10	Der Brand von Persepolis	1993	Amsterdam: Hakkert	G. Wirth	German	3

#	Title	Year	Publisher	Editor/Author	Language	No.
11	Collected Studies III	1994	Amsterdam: Hakkert	N.G.L. Hammond	English	19
	Collected Studies IV	1997			English	13
12	Alexander the Great: Ancient and Modern Perspectives	1995	Lexington, MA: Heath	J. Roisman, ed.	English	15
13	Alexander der Grosse	1998	Bonn: Habelt	W. Will, ed.	German (5) English (4)	9
14	Alexander the Great in Fact and Fiction	2000	Oxford: Oxford U.P.	A. B. Bosworth and E. Baynham, eds.	English	10
15	Brill's Companion to Alexander the Great	2003	Leiden-Boston: Brill	J. Roisman, ed.	English	13
16	Crossroads to History: The Age of Alexander	2003	Claremont, CA: Regina Books	W. Heckel and L. A. Tritle, eds.	English	11
17	Alexander the Great: A reader	2003	London-New York: Routledge	I. Worthington, ed.	English	25
18	Alexander's Empire: Formulation to Decay	2007	Claremont, CA: Regina Books	W. Heckel, L. A. Tritle, and P. Wheatley, eds.	English	16
19	Special Section on Alexander the Great	2007	Classical World 100/4: 417–40	—	English	4
20	Alexander the Great: A New History	2009	Oxford and New York: Blackwell	W. Heckel and L. A. Tritle, eds.	English	16
21	Alexander and His Successors: Essays from the Antipodes	2009	Claremont: CA: Regina Books	P. Wheatley and R. Hannah, eds.	English	17
22	Collected Papers on Alexander the Great	2009	London-New York: Routledge	E. Badian	English	16
23	Philip II and Alexander III: Father, Son, and Dunasteia	Forthc.	—	E. Carney, org.	English	28

ing (wrongly) that European studies of the subject have ceased entirely. When in 2004 W. Heckel posed the question, "What's new in Alexander studies?" he might as well have asked "What's new *in English* in Alexander studies?" as, with a single exception, no "foreign" study was mentioned in the entire article.[15]

(ii) Also worth noting is the rate at which publications appear: three volumes of collected essays between 2003 and 2010, and no fewer than seven colloquia on Alexander the Great between 1998 and 2009, making a total of ten books in ten years. And that is without counting the hundreds of books and articles published in the same period.[16] This exponential growth should not lead one to think that all these *recent* works are truly *new*. The manuals are certainly useful for teaching, but—with a few exceptions—structure and themes are virtually identical from one book to the next, certain articles are reprinted again and again, and major aspects of historical research are totally absent or not given the attention due them. This is particularly the case with the economic aspects of the conquest, apart from the reprinting of passages by Wilcken from 1931 (B3, B8). Just one very short article deals with Alexander's monetary policy (B9),[17] even though this is the one area where there is new evidence and interpretations have seen a striking transformation.

This state of affairs may explain the tone of a recent review:[18] "In Alexanderland, scholarship remains largely un-

---

[15] http://www.apaclassics.org/outreach/amphora/2004/Amphora3.1.pdf.

[16] In the book by M. Kets de Vries and E. Engellau (nonspecialists) published in 2004 (see above n. 4), the authors cite the round figure of "30,000 books and articles" published at the time of their writing (p. xxii, n. 1). I have no idea where they obtained this figure.

[17] At this time, its author, the late Martin Price, had already planned to publish his great work on the subject (1991).

[18] J. Davidson, "Bonkers about Boys," *London Review of Books* (November 11, 2001: http://www.lrb.co.uk/v23/n21/davi02.html), together with A. B. Bosworth's

touched by the influences which have transformed history and classics since 1945." The chosen target (*Fact and Fiction*, B13) is not perhaps the best for such a dismissive judgment, and it requires some qualification, but in general terms several of the reviewer's remarks have hit home. There are very real gaps in current Alexander histories.[19] G. T. Griffith had already drawn attention to one of the lacunae in 1966 (B2, ix), when he deplored the absence of any full study of Alexander's ability (or not) to transform the situation he found in the empire. Sadly, forty years on, this question has still not received the attention it deserves—either in most of the manuals or in the specialist colloquia, which I have just discussed.[20]

(iii) Research into the historiography of Alexander is strikingly limited. Despite the studies by Bikerman and Momigliano, it continues to be asserted as a self-evident truth that the study of Alexander only begins with Droysen's *Alexander* of 1833.[21] This is simply not the case. If we are to refresh our historiographical methods and aims, it will be essential to trace the elaboration and evolution of the dominant image of Alexander the Great from the eighteenth to the twentieth century.[22] Such a study must be conducted in

---

response (*London Review of Books*, January 3, 2002), and that of W. Heckel in the article cited above (n. 15).

[19] See also the remarks by M. Flower in B19 (2007): 419–20.

[20] On this, see my discussion in B20 (2009), chapter 9.

[21] The bibliography on Droysen is too vast to cite, and is largely in languages other than English. Bravo's book (*Philologie, histoire, philosophie de l'histoire. Étude sur J.-G. Droysen historien de l'Antiquité*, Wroclaw-Warsaw-Cracow 1968) remains the fundamental study. In English, see the convenient and recent discussion by A. B. Bosworth, "Alexander the Great and the Creation of the Hellenistic Age," in G. Bugh, ed., *The Cambridge Companion to the Hellenistic World*, Cambridge 2006: 9–26; and "Johann Gustav Droysen, Alexander the Great and the creation of the Hellenistic Age," in B 21 (2009): 1–27.

[22] See my observations in *The Oxford Handbook of Hellenic Studies*, Oxford, 2009: 77–85, and the bibliography there. I have been working on this topic for several years, and am currently preparing a book on the subject.

conjunction with an analysis of the contemporary European images of Persia and the "Orient."[23] Historiography is not a substitute for history, but it helps the process of reflection on issues and their assessment. It makes it possible to see more clearly the circumstances in which this or that thesis emerged and why it may reappear without any apparent reason. For example, a "novel" thesis has recently been resurrected, condemning Alexander for marching against Egypt after Issus rather than pursuing Darius. The king, according to this, was moved to do so by his overwhelming desire (*pothos*) to consult the oracle of Amun. We are asked to see here an example of Alexander's strategic mistakes and proof of his "irrationality."[24] In fact, this discussion began at the end of the seventeenth century, and spread in the context of the "canonical history" of the eighteenth century (*e.g.*, Rollin and Mably in France; Prideaux and Shuckford in England). Its objective was to condemn Alexander's "extraordinary rashness" and his rejection of Darius' diplomatic overtures.[25] (Voltaire had already settled the matter brilliantly!) Plainly, this type of moralizing history has come back with vigor in the last fifteen years.

(iv) Of course, any progress is limited by the scant nature of the sources, apart from the Graeco-Roman literary

[23] Apart from Briant, *Darius dans l'ombre*, see also my "Alexander and the Persian Empire: Between 'Decline' and 'Renovation'," in B20 (2009): 171–88; "Le thème de la 'décadence perse' dans l'historiographie européenne du XVIIIe siècle: remarques préliminaires sur la genèse d'un mythe," in L. Bodiou et al, eds., *Mélanges Pierre Brulé*, Rennes 2009: 19–38.

[24] E. F. Bloedow, "Egypt in Alexander's Scheme of Things," *Quaderni Urbinati di Cultura Classica* 77/2 (2004): 75–99. The writer begins his investigation with Droysen, but the discussion of this theme has a much longer history. The same thesis is also found in a very naïve article by I. Worthington, "How Great Was Alexander?" *AHB* 13/2 (1999): 39–55, esp. 45–46 (= B17 [2003]: 308); note F. L. Holt's justified criticism (B17: 322).

[25] See my article, "Montesquieu, Mably et Alexandre le Grand: aux sources de l'histoire hellénistique," *Revue Montesquieu* 8 (2005–2006): 151–85 (162–77).

ones, that document the history of Alexander directly. The most recently found and published piece of evidence is a "medallion," which is said to have come from the treasure of Mir Zakah in Afghanistan (Fig. 10a-b).[26] It is of gold alloy and of a weight similar to a double daric (16.75 grams). The reverse of this unique medallion shows an elephant walking to the right, with the letters BA (standing for *Basileos Alexandrou*, according to Bopearachchi, although he also expresses some well-founded doubts). On the obverse is "the head of Alexander, covered with an elephant's scalp; he wears an aegis, or the shield of Zeus, and the 'ram's horns' of Ammon." Some features are comparable to the coin series known as the "elephant coinage," the dating and significance of which remain highly contentious (Fig. 3).[27] The "medallion" is thought to have been struck in India in Alexander's lifetime, after his victory over Poros. It would then be the only contemporary portrait of Alexander, and would have served as a prototype for the coins struck by Ptolemy using his image (Fig. 10C). It would also bear testimony to Alexander's divinization in his lifetime.

Unfortunately, some specialists express serious doubts about the medallion's authenticity,[28] while others are critical of the first editor's presentation and argumentation.[29] The

[26] O. Bopearachchi and P. Flandrin, *Le portrait d'Alexandre le Grand*, Monaco and Paris 2005. (The subtitle, *Histoire d'une découverte pour l'humanité*, is needlessly pompous.) An international colloquium on the object was organized by Bopearachchi at the École Normale Supérieure (Paris) on March 26, 2007. The proceedings are not yet published.

[27] See the brief discussion of the issue in Le Rider, "A Mysterious Group of Silver Coins," *Alexander the Great*: 247–52; and a detailed discussion in F. L. Holt, *Alexander the Great and the Mystery of the Elephant Medallions*, Berkeley, CA 2003.

[28] E.g., K. Dahmen, *The Legend of Alexander the Great on Greek and Roman Coins*, London 2007: 9 ("of questionable authenticity").

[29] See the recent study of S. Bhandare, "Not Just a Pretty Face: Interpretations of Alexander's Numismatic Imagery in the Hellenistic East," in H. P. Ray and D. T. Potts, eds., *Memory as History: The Legacy of Alexander in Asia*, New Delhi 2007:

Fig. 10A–B. The gold "Alexander Medallion" from the Mir Zakah (Afghanistan) Hoard, discovered in 1992. A (obverse): Head of Alexander wearing an elephant's scalp. B (reverse): elephant. Photo: copyright Osmund Bopearachchi.

Fig. 10C: Alexander with an elephant's scalp on his head, on a coin struck by the satrap Ptolemy after 323 BC. From P. Francke and M. Hirmer, *La monnaie grecque*, Paris (1966): Pl. 217, no. 29.

dossier as a whole is a kind of paradigm of the uncertainties and assumptions that beset current studies of Alexander.

Having expressed these criticisms, it seems to me more constructive to emphasize recent advances, which means repeating an earlier observation about the evidence.[30] This is

208–56, who inserts the medallion into the long-term debate about the "elephant coinage."

[30] This is an observation that I have made before, more than once; see most recently, *The Oxford Handbook of Hellenic Studies*, Oxford 2009: 82–84.

simply the fact that, as Alexander is situated at the conflu-ence of Macedonian and Achaemenid history, the study of his career has fed both of those disciplines and it must in turn be fed by them. The unprecedented development over the last thirty years of research both on the Argead kingdom and on the empire of the Great Kings has brought, and con-tinues to bring, a regular harvest of unpublished documents that raise new questions, which provoke new ways of ap-proaching the history of Alexander.

We can gain an impression of how things stand by looking at what was, at the time (1948), the first real his-torical synthesis of the Persian empire, namely A. T. Olm-stead's *History of the Persian Empire*. The book was published posthumously thanks to his colleagues at the Oriental Insti-tute of Chicago and the devotion of his daughter.[31] It ends with an almost lyrical report on the recent strides made in the empire's history:

> For the whole empire period, archaeologist and philologist have come to the aid of the historian. . . . No longer are we entirely dependent on Greek "classics" for the story of Per-sia's relations with the West. . . . Close to twenty-three centuries have elapsed since Alexander burned Persepolis; now, at last, through the united effort of archaeologist, phi-lologist, and historian, Achaemenid Persia has risen from the dead. (524)

In order to underscore his point, Olmstead contrasted the pro-fusion of evidence relating to the Persian empire with what he considered the lamentable state of evidence for Macedon:

[31] See the Foreword by George Cameron (p. v), who was publishing, in the same year, the first volume of the Persepolis tablets (*Persepolis Treasury Tablets*, Chicago, IL 1948).

The Macedonia of Alexander has disappeared, almost without trace. Its older capital Aegae is a malaria-ridden site and nothing more. . . . The tombs of the Macedonian rulers, where Alexander had thought to be gathered to his fathers, have never been found; his own capital, Pella, is a mass of shapeless ruins. . . . But Persepolis stands to this day. (522–23)

Since Olmstead wrote these lines, Macedonian history has developed enormously, thanks to the joint efforts of archaeologists and epigraphists. We could in fact borrow his words on Persian history and apply them to Macedon: "No longer are we entirely dependent on Greek 'classics' for the story of Macedonian relations with the South!" Or we might go one better and quote Miltiades Hatzopoulos, one of the protagonists of this profound historiographical shift, in a recent work:

Half a century after the start of systematic, large scale excavations, the huge labour by archaeologists, who have dragged from the earth ruins hidden in the past, and the patient work of all the scholars who have concentrated the expertise on their finds, have revealed an inhabited land that had been *terra incognita* and given a face to the people, enigmatic until that point, whom Alexander led to the ends of the earth.[32]

Hatzopoulos' statement seems to echo, sixty years later, that of Olmstead. Taken together, they tell us quite simply that the Macedon of Philip and the empire of Artaxerxes III/IV

[32] M. Hatzopoulos, *La Macédoine. Géographie historique, langue, culte et croyances, institutions*, Paris 2006: 93; see also, M. Hatzopoulos, *Macedonian Institutions under the Kings* I (1996): 37–42, and his synthesis, "L'État macédonien antique: un nouveau visage," *CRAI* 1997: 7–25.

are now open to the gaze of historians working on Alexander and Darius.

༝ྕ᠍ᢓ᠍ᢦ

Historians of Alexander will not be surprised by the first part of that observation. "The Macedonian Background" is an obligatory chapter in their publications, and some are remarkable connoisseurs of Macedon.[33] I do not intend to give here a description of the most recent Macedonian discoveries. I shall limit my comments to two finds, one archaeological, the other epigraphic. It is well known that when discussing the necropolis at Aegae (the bibliography on which is immense, bordering on the uncontrollable), discussions of the dating of Tomb II (Philip II or III?) automatically involve discussion of the cross-cultural influences between Macedon and the Achaemenid world. Does the motif of the lion hunt belong to Macedonian tradition or does it indicate a borrowing from the Achaemenid world transferred to Macedon in an almost instant response to Alexander's conquest?[34]

[33] I am thinking particularly of Eugene Borza. Apart from his general book on Macedon (*In the Shadow of Olympus: The Emergence of Macedon*, Princeton, NJ 1990), he has published two collections of his articles on Macedon (Association of Ancient Historians, 1995 and 1999), as well as editing a volume of essays by various authors on Alexander (B3) and providing an "Introduction to Alexander Studies," as the preface to a reissue of the English translation of Wilcken (*Alexander the Great*, New York 1967: ix–xxviii); see also his contribution to a debate on teaching Alexander history (B12 [2007]: 436–40). On Borza's work, see recently T. Howe and J. Reames, eds., *Macedonian Legacies: Studies in Ancient Macedonian History and Culture in Honour of E. N. Borza*, Claremont, CA 2008. See also the following footnote.

[34] See most recently, O. Palagia and E. Borza, "The Chronology of the Macedonian Royal Tombs at Vergina," *Jahreshefte des Deutschen Archäologischen Instituts* 122 (2007): 81–124 (90–103), with a full bibliography. On the Macedonian and Persian traditions of the hunt in the epoch of Alexander, see also my remarks in *AchHist* VIII (1994): 302–310, P. Vidal-Naquet's contribution (now sadly forgotten), "Alexandre et les chasseurs noirs," in *Arrien entre deux mondes* (Arrien, His-

The many new inscriptions relate largely to the Hellenistic period. Their publication history can be followed in the section "Macédoine" (under the name Hatzopoulos) of the *Bulletin Épigraphique* of the *Revue des Études Grecques*, beginning in 1987.[35] Alexander's reign is illuminated by a number of inscriptions.[36] These provide evidence of a hero-cult in honor of Hephaestion,[37] and a dossier on relations between Alexander and the Greek sanctuaries,[38] but we must give prominence here to an inscription from the city of Philippi. It was discovered in 1936, but first published by Vatin only in 1984; since then it has been reedited several times.[39] There are problems with the restoration of the text and with its historical interpretation, as a result of which considerable controversy has arisen, in particular between Hammond and Badian.[40] Several interlinked lines of enquiry are raised by this document: a) that concerning the precise territory of the new city founded by Philip in eastern Macedon, and thus the geography and topography of the

---

toire d'Alexandre, trans. P. Savinel, Paris 1984: 309–94): 355–65, and E. Carney, "Hunting and the Macedonian Elite: Sharing the Rivalry of the Chase," in D. Ogden, ed., *The Hellenistic World: New Perspectives*, Classical Press of Wales and Duckworth 2002: 59–80.

[35] The *Bulletin Épigraphique* 1987–2001 has been reprinted as four volumes (Paris 2007).

[36] See R. M. Errington's analytical study, "Neue epigraphische Belege für Makedonien zur Zeit Alexanders des Grossen," in B13 (1998): 77–90.

[37] *Bulletin Épigraphique* 1992, no. 309, and M. Mari in *Studi Ellenistici* XX (2008): 230–31 and n. 27 (dedication on a stela from Pydna, ca. 315–300 BC).

[38] See now, M. Mari, *Al di là di Olimpo. Macedoni e grandi santuari della Grecia dall'età arcaica al primo Ellenismo* (Meletemata 34), Athens 2002: 203–262; see the epigraphical analysis on pp. 227–30 of relations between Olympias and Delphi during her son's campaign, which complements E. Carney's work, *Olympias* (2006): 49.

[39] See M. Hatzopoulos, *Macedonian Institutions* II (1996), no. 6 (25–28); S. Ager, *Interstate Arbitrations in the Greek World (337–90 B.C.)*, Berkeley, CA 1996, no. 5 (47–49).

[40] The debates can be followed via the *Bulletin Épigraphique* 1987, no. 714; 1988, no. 495; 1990, no. 495; 1991, no. 417; 1993, no. 356; and 1994, no. 436.

region; b) that concerning intervention by the royal administration (well attested in other kingdoms) as the arbiter on
frontiers and thus of relations between kings and cities at
the time of Philip and Alexander;[41] c) questions of Macedonian administration in Alexander's absence, and the relations between the royal camp while on the move and his
kingdom in Europe (including communications between
them); d) and finally, the question of Alexander's territorial
objectives at the time of his departure from Macedon.

This last is precisely the larger perspective that Hatzopoulos wished to emphasize in a 1997 article.[42] On the basis
of his readings and the connections he makes with the historical context, he insists that we have here proof that Alexander
changed his plans abruptly at Persepolis. Instead of turning
back to Macedon (as, according to the author, he had intended), he decided to continue the war against Darius.

We can obviously either accept or reject that hypothesis—and this is not the place to go into a detailed analysis.[43] But, given the major impact such a historical revision
has on the much discussed problem of the burning of Persepolis (see above, chapter V), it is very odd that the inscription is only cited in that context in three of the articles included in the colloquia on Alexander (B13: 82–86),[44] of

[41] This point is discussed by Farraguna in B15 (1998): 111–12.

[42] "Alexandre en Perse. La revanche et l'empire," *ZPE* 116 (1997): 41–52; the
author had clearly stated his interpretation in the *Bulletin Épigraphique* 1987, no.
714; his view is repeated in no. 282. (1998): nn. 36 and 39.

[43] I have never concealed my very serious reservations; cf. the 2002 and 2005
French editions of this book (p. 57, n. 1) and Briant, *History* (2002): 1047–48. It
seems to me that the dating of the boundary marking (entrusted to Philotas and
Leonnatos) to a time preceding 334 is much more persuasive than the very complex scenario presented by Hatzopoulos. See the similar criticisms of *e.g.*, Errington
(n. 36, above) and Ager (n. 39, above).

[44] The detailed epigraphic and historical discussion by R. M. Errington, counter-
ing the readings and interpretations of Hatzopoulos (for his reply, see *Bulletin
Épigraphique* 1998, no. 281).

which two simply refer to it in passing (B14, B15);[45] odd too that the dossier has never been the subject of a full examination in any of the numerous collective volumes published between 1965 and 2009 (table 2). As far as I am aware, neither does it figure in any of the more recent monographs and articles dealing with the Persepolis affair, and it is absent as well from a recent colloquium on the teaching of Alexander's history in American universities (B19 [2007]). And yet this is a document that raises important educational and epistemological issues relevant to the question of "documentary proof," which is so important in our profession, and to the interaction of literary and epigraphic sources. It is of infinitely greater value to the historian than, for example, yet another account of that elusive phantom figure Cleitarchus.

When we turn to the place occupied by the Persian empire in the current historiography of Alexander, the situation is somewhat different. There is often no analysis of the Achaemenid adversary at all, and certainly none of any depth. The history of the conquest is organized exclusively around the figure of Alexander and his itinerary. Whereas the nineteenth-century works (from Droysen in 1833 onwards), as well as the eighteenth-century manuals, always included an introductory chapter on the Achaemenid state, this has disappeared, and/or the Achaemenid sources are ignored. It is as if, for example, a French historian of the Franco-Prussian War of 1870 had failed to take account of the situation in Prussia and the German lands and centered his whole narra-

---

[45] M. Flower (B3 [2000]: 116, n. 85) observes briefly that the literary sources do not agree with Hatzopoulos' interpretation, but does not treat the inscription itself; Brosius in B15 (2003): 185, n. 25, refers to it indirectly while analyzing the Persepolis affair.

tive on Napoleon III while forgetting Bismarck! Paradoxically, there has been more interest recently in the figure of Darius[46] (a biographical approach to whom is literally impossible in the absence of documentation),[47] but in the process the Persian empire he reigned over, about which we have more and more information, has been forgotten.

Further, more often than not these articles tend towards a kind of "rehabilitation" of the last Great King, by simplistically reversing the perspective. The task of the historian, however, is not to create a history of "victims," any more than to write a history of "conquerors."[48] Rather, we must try to reconstruct a global history, in other words one that is complex, enfolding multiple perspectives. While the ancient sources have glorified Alexander and his conquests, the historian should not feel obliged to go to the other extreme and display, naïvely, a "compassionate admiration" of the Persian empire, comparable to the attitude supposedly evinced by Alexander when he found Darius' corpse![49] Does it need repeating that a reconsideration of Achaemenid history is not the same thing as either the "rehabilitation" of Darius or an exaltation of the grandeur of his empire? The objective is a *reevaluation* (the scientific approach), not the *rehabilitation* (the moralizing approach) of Achaemenid history. Our aim is to understand better what

[46] Cf. J. Seibert, "Dareios III," in B7, I (1987): 437–56; E. Badian, "Darius III," *HSClPh* 100 (2000): 241–68 [= B22, 2010]; E. Garvin, "Darius III and the Homeland Defense," in B16 [2003]: 87–112; see also C. Nylander, "Darius III—The Coward King. Point and Counterpoint," in B9 (1993): 145–59.

[47] See Briant, *Darius dans l'ombre*, esp. p. 530f. on Nylander's idea in the wake of Widengren.

[48] *Pace* J. D. Grainger, *Alexander the Great Failure: The Collapse of the Macedonian Empire* (2007): 189–90.

[49] On this image, see Briant, *Darius dans l'ombre*, chapter 11: "Mort et transfiguration" (pp. 487ff.). It is this lachrymose tradition that G. Grote denounced as "almost tragic pathos" (cited *ibid.*: 103–104).

state the empire was in when it was attacked and invaded by the Macedonian army.

At the same time, the accelerating development of Achaemenid history has obviously not been completely ignored. One recent writer, who presents herself as a nonspecialist on Alexander but is anxious to take an original approach, has chosen to set Alexander and the conquest into the Macedonian context vis-à-vis Achaemenid history.[50] Reflecting on how we should teach the history of Alexander today, Flower expressed the same idea:[51]

> Alexander's achievement and its consequences must be understood against the background not just of earlier Greek and Macedonian history, but also of Persian history.

One reviewer emphasized that book's appeal as follows:

> As such, the approach is welcome, for much of the excellent scholarship on the development of the Macedonian kingdom to the death of Philip II . . . and on the nature of the Achaemenid empire on the eve of the Macedonian invasion . . . tends to be beyond the reach of many students.[52]

However, what needs to be stressed is the marked and highly revealing imbalance between the information on Macedon and that on the Achaemenid empire, that was brought into play by the author of the book: her pages on Achaemenid history (159–73) are extremely general and not really linked to the history of the Macedonian conquest.[53]

---

[50] C. Thomas, *Alexander the Great and His World*, Oxford 2007: esp. p. x.

[51] M. Flower in B19 (2007): 420.

[52] E. Mackil, CR 58/1 (2008): 201. (Despite Flower's identical observation [see the previous note], I am not convinced that this problem is exclusively one experienced by students.)

[53] The same is true, for example, of P. Cartledge's book despite its promising subtitle: *Alexander the Great: The Hunt for a New Past*, London 2004: 40–46.

It would seem, then, that the recent advances in Achaemenid historiography are not always correctly evaluated and taken fully into account.[54] Flower, in an otherwise interesting presentation (B19 [2007]: 422, n. 20), rather oddly described the British Museum exhibition of 2005 as a "major revisionist exhibition," because, in his opinion, its aim was "to rehabilitate Persian culture." But this was hardly the first time that an exhibition devoted to the cultural patrimony of Achaemenid Iran (which stood in little need of "rehabilitation") had been organized, and we did not have to wait until 2005 to know that the Persians had "a sophisticated and interesting culture of their own." With its negative connotations, the adjective "revisionist" is exceptionally problematic and misleading. There is also the danger that nonspecialists and students might confuse this with the other "revisionist school" (or rather one identified as such!) in the historiography of Alexander. In that context, the adjective generally describes those writers who have been influenced by the debunking of Tarn's 1933 theses (B1 [1966]: 243–86) by Badian in 1958 (B1 [1966] : 287–306, B22 [2010]); however, not all authors who distance themselves from Tarn's approach would consider themselves "revisionists"![55]

❧

This is perhaps the appropriate place to suggest what we can expect from the contribution of Achaemenid history, and at the same time to stress its limitations, so as to avoid any

---

[54] See J. Lendering, BMCR 2008.09.62., and "Let's Abandon Achaemenid Studies!" July 2008: http.livius.org/opinion/opinion 0012.html; see also V. Vashakize's excessively aggressive response (together with others), BMCRI 2009.02.02. I stress that such a polemical exchange gives a distorted, not to say caricatured, image of the state of Achaemenid history today.

[55] E.g., Bosworth, *Alexander and the East:* p. v.

misunderstandings.[56] One important point to note: it will never be possible to write a narrative history of Alexander from the perspective of the conquered, as we have neither continuous accounts nor even partial ones from Persia, Babylonia, or Egypt.

(i) As we have seen, Babylonian texts are the most useful. A well-known Babylonian tablet gives us a detailed image of the weeks from the Battle of Arbela to Alexander's entry into Babylon and of the conditions surrounding his acceptance by the Babylonian elites.[57] This document can, in turn, be compared to the Graeco-Roman texts, whose narrative style adds complementary and/or contradictory elements.[58] However, the meaning of cuneiform texts is not always clear. For example, the combined mention of Darius, Alexander, and Bessos in a Babylonian chronicle of this period remains hard to understand, and it cannot provide unambiguous evidence.[59]

Other sets of tablets, of a rather more pedestrian nature, give information on variations in the levels of the Euphrates and on regular work carried out on the Pallukatu (Pallacopas) canal. In its way, such information can be very helpful to historians trying to understand the nature of Alexander's work in 324/3 on Babylonia's rivers and canals.[60]

(ii) A single coin of Mazday/Mazaeus has given rise to a hypothesis on the maintenance of Persian positions in

[56] See on this the apt remarks of J.-P. Stronk, BMCR 2005.07.35.

[57] Texts in R. Van der Spek, AchHist XIII (2003); 289–346; A. Kuhrt, The Persian Empire I (2007): 447–48.

[58] To the familiar texts (Arrian, Quintus Curtius, etc.) P. Goukowsky's recent article ("Le cortège des 'rois de Babylone,'" Bulletin of the Asia Institute 12 (1998): 69–77) adds the evidence of Iamblichus; but its late date raises problems.

[59] Cf. R. Van der Spek, AchHist XIII (2003): 303–308.

[60] Briant, Studi Ellenistici XX (2008): 204–207 (with references to the Assyriological studies).

Syria after the Battle of Issus. But even if the coin is indeed authentic, it should not really be used in that way.[61]

(iii) The Aramaic papyri, seal impressions (Fig. 11), and coins found in the Wadi Daliyeh (about 30 km from Jericho), which have been known for half a century, are thought to relate to the anti-Macedonian revolt of 331 known from Quintus Curtius.[62] The assumption is that well-to-do Samarians, on the occasion of the revolt, fled the city and took refuge in the caves together with their families and private archives. But Quintus Curtius' passage can also be linked with passages in late authors, as well as to an inscription and coin from the Roman period. Putting all these together, they would attest to a joint action by Alexander and Perdiccas in Samaria and Gerasa.[63] This body of material is particularly interesting in that it allows us to gauge the extent of our ignorance. By following the progress of the Macedonian army step by step and focusing on Alexander's personality and conduct, the literary sources tend to leave in the shade the "secondary" campaigns, which were undertaken alongside the offensives by the bulk of the army.[64]

(iv) The Lydian inscriptions dating to one year of Alexander's reign provide no direct information, and it is dif-

[61] The problem is discussed by Lemaire, in Briant and Joannès, eds., *La Transition:* 407.

[62] IV.6.9–10 (above, chapter I); see already Briant, *History* (2002): 713–16 and 1016 (with bibliography) and, since then, M.J.W. Leith, *Wadi Daliyeh I: The Wadi Daliyeh Seal Impressions* (Discoveries in the Judaean Desert XXIV), Oxford 1997, esp. pp. 3–35, and D. M. Gropp, *Wadi Daliyeh II: The Samaria Papyri from the Wadi Daliyeh* (Discoveries in the Judaean Desert XXVIII), Oxford 2001, esp. pp. 3–32. The latest papyrus (WDSP 1) dates to year 0 of Darius III and year 2 of his (unnamed) predecessor (March 19, 335), and was drawn up "in Samaria the citadel (*birtha*), which is in Samaria the province (*medinah*)."

[63] See H. Seyrig, "Alexandre le Grand, fondateur de Gerasa," (1965) in *Antiquités Syriennes* VIè série, Paris 1966: 141–44.

[64] Apart from Quintus Curtius, IV.8.9–10 (Samaria), see IV.1.4 (Parmenion's expedition in Syria) and IV.2.24, 3.1 (Alexander's move from Tyre to deal with revolts in Lebanon): Atkinson, *Commentary* I (1980); 300–301, 369–70.

Fig. 11. The "Persian Hero" grappling with flanking animals, from a Samarian seal impression. Drawing and description in M.J.W. Leith, *Wadi Daliyeh I: The Wadi Daliyeh Seal Impressions* (*Discoveries in the Judaean Desert* XXIV), Oxford 1997, no. WD 17, 209–210.

ficult (as is the case with some Babylonian documents) to determine with any certainty which king of the name Alexander is meant.[65]

(v) The same problem—*i.e.*, which Alexander is meant by the designation the "reigning king"—divides specialists dealing with some of the Aramaic administrative documents from Idumaea. Is it Alexander the Great or his son?[66] If it is Alexander the Great, then the ostracon AL

[65] See T. Boiy, *Kadmos* 44 (2005); 165–74.
[66] Different positions are taken by Lemaire in Briant and Joannès, eds., *La Transition*: 416–19, and Boiy, in *La Transition*: 48, 58–63; cf. Briant, "Empire of Darius" in B20 (2009): 152–55, with bibliography.

38*, dated to 16 Siwan, year 2 of Alexander the king, would be of June 26, 331, when Alexander was returning from Egypt and moving towards the Euphrates. The problem with this is that it supposes the existence of an Alexander era specific to the regions of Palestine. As a result the assumption in most recent studies is that the Alexander of the Idumaean ostraca is Alexander IV.[67]

(vi) The new Aramaic documents from Bactria are extremely important, particularly in relation to the issue of the transition from the Achaemenid to the Macedonian period. Nevertheless, they still pose some problems as to exactly how they link up with the history of Darius, Alexander, and Bessos. Three types of documents demand consideration in this connection:

(a) Most important is the fact that we have here a set of documents dated to one year of Darius III, namely 18 wooden sticks recording debts, all from year 3 of Darius (D1–18).[68]

(b) A document (C1) is dated "In the month of Kislev, year 1 of Arta[xerxes] the King." It records the delivery of various products to a certain Bayasa, "when he passed from Bactra to Varnu." The editors propose to identify him with Bessos, in the course of his flight from Bactra, and suggest that Bessos is also the reigning king Arta-xerxes. The date would then be November–December 330. This is very exciting evidence, as it would give us a

[67] See in particular B. Porten and A. Yardeni, "The Chronology of the Idumaean Ostraka in the Decade or so after the Death of Alexander the Great and Its Relevance for Historical Events," in M. Cogan and D. Kahn, eds., *Treasures on Camel's Humps: Historical and Literary Studies from the Ancient Near East Presented to Israel Eph'al*, Jerusalem 2008: 237–50.

[68] Documents dated to Darius III in the empire are collected in Briant, *Darius dans l'ombre:* 62–64 and 562–63 (together with a preliminary discussion of the Bactrian documents, p. 63 and n. 19).

direct insight into the period when Bessos was fleeing before Alexander. But it seems rather odd that in one and the same document, the same individual is called both by his own and his regnal name.[69]

(c) Another document (C3) is certainly dated to Alexander's reign, as follows: "On the 15th of Siwan, year 7 of Alexander the King" (col.1, ll.1–2), which is June 8, 324 according to the editors. Again it is an administrative text recording the transfer of a variety of products (wheat, barley, millet, etc.) as rations over a period of three months (Siwan, Tammuz, and Ab), from storehouses at Airavant and Varaina. Unfortunately neither location is known.[70]

The proposed dating introduces information that is new. In Babylonia, the contemporary cuneiform documents are dated exclusively in terms of Alexander's regnal years in Macedon, for which reason there are no tablets dating from years 1 to 6 of Alexander, as these correspond to years 1 to 6 of Darius. The change from Achaemenid to Macedonian control is marked by the accession year (known as year 0) of Alexander, which lasts just to the next Babylonian year, i.e., April 3, 330. At this point, Alexander's year 7 begins and continues to Nisan, that is March of 329.[71] Even though no official document records them, all events from the pursuit of Darius to Alexander's arrival in Bactria at the end of winter/beginning of spring 329 fall into this very year 7. It is also

---

[69] For a presentation, translation, and detailed commentary on this document, see S. Shaked, "De Khulmi à Nikhšapaya: les données des nouveaux documents araméens de Bactres sur la toponymie de la région (IVe siècle av. notre ère)," *CRAI* November–December 2003: 1517–35. See my doubts on this dating in B20 (2009): 147, n. 28.

[70] Shaked, *Satrape de Bactriane* (2003): 17–18.

[71] See Briant and Joannès, eds., *La Transition:* 42–49 (Boiy) and 104–108 (Joannès).

in year 7 that, theoretically, the proclamation of Bessos as King Artaxerxes falls. If we follow this dating method, then the date of the Bactrian document would be June 15, 330. The editors consider that impossible, as Alexander had not yet arrived in Bactria; they have, therefore, chosen to date it to June 8, 324. This seems logical, but it is surprising that the Bactrian chancellery should choose to begin Alexander's reign according to a Babylonian computation, which recent studies show was never used in Babylonia itself.[72]

⚜

In conclusion, I should like to turn to another instance, which illustrates the importance of the Achaemenid context for reconstructing Alexander's campaigns. In 1978, D. W. Engels published a study of Alexander's logistics, which was rightly welcomed as presenting a new and virtually unexamined aspect of Alexander's history.[73] He observed that the success of a long-term military expedition was inconceivable without the logistical planning necessary to ensure the resupply of resources all along the route of its advance. Alexander's success thus depended as much on the logistical measures he took in the course of his campaigns as on the stocks of provisions he might find and mobilize in the lands he was traversing and conquering.

This meant that Achaemenid resources were absolutely indispensable to Alexander—and not merely agricul-

---

[72] Given that Alexander on leaving Parthia and Areia decided to pursue Bessos to Bactria from the moment of the latter's proclamation as king, before being compelled to take the road back to Areia (Arrian III.23–25.1–6), we might be tempted to think that he was recognized as king from his year 7 onwards in accordance with the Macedonian pattern; but the suggestion is not free of problems.

[73] *Alexander the Great and the Logistics of the Macedonian Army*, Berkeley, CA 1978; on working out the rations needed for animals, see the critical comments by M. Gabrielli, *Le cheval dans l'empire achéménide*, Istanbul 2006.

tural products but also the institutions established by the imperial administration to create reserves and ensure their maintenance. A passage in the pseudo-Aristotelian *Oikonomika* (II.2.38) illustrates brilliantly how Alexander's administration co-opted Achaemenid measures for maintaining reserves in the magazines along the royal roads. When Alexander made use of the Achaemenid road system, he knew well how "to turn to his own advantage the logistics the Persian authority had established to ensure its survival."[74]

In this respect, Engels' use of the Graeco-Roman sources leaves something to be desired. On p. 72, for example, he declares that Persis was "sparse and rugged," for which his sole witness is Herodotus 9.22 in a passage created to make the point that people who are poor are *perforce* ready to become conquerors! Other evidence, some of it from eyewitnesses, provides far more precise and credible information.[75] What is more, R. T. Hallock's edition of the Persepolis Fortification Tablets (1969–1978) was already published and readily accessible at this point. Both agricultural production and the raising of flocks in Persis were extensive, and, in 330, there were certainly a substantial number of garrisoned storehouses, which Alexander could use to feed his army.[76] It is also a structural weakness of Engels's book that he rarely discusses the grain and other food reserves held in the satrapies, a system well attested by many Achaemenid documents, as well as by the classical sources.[77] As a result of these omissions, Engels overstresses the explanatory (and often exclusive) value of the (of course, im-

---

[74] Briant, *History* (2002): 317–74 (373); on the ps.-Aristotle passage, see Briant, "Empire of Darius," in B20 (2009): 166–67.

[75] Diodorus XVII.67.3, XIX.21.2–3; Quintus Curtius V.4.6–9.

[76] See already my observations in Briant, *Rois, tributs et paysans*: 202–10, 329, 331–45; *History*: 733–37.

[77] Cf. Xenophon, *Anab.* III.4.17, 31 (strategic materials).

portant) diverse modes of transport, and the (no less important) dates of harvests.

Yet one further example: not a single account of the Macedonian expedition in Bactria-Sogdiana refers to the existence of the region's highly developed irrigation system, known from excavations (of which Engels is aware, pp. 98–100). The presence of irrigation agriculture must have dictated the choice of sites for colonization and urbanization made by Alexander and his successors.[78] In addition to the archaeological evidence,[79] the more recent Aramaic documents from Bactria (discussed above) provide extremely important information. Dating from the end of the Achaemenid era and Alexander's reign, several of these Aramaic texts attest the existence of official storehouses, filled with foodstuffs of all kinds, on which the administration could draw to feed men and animals (fodder).[80] It also had at its disposal numerous pack animals (donkeys and camels). This new material helps, however indirectly, to throw light on Alexander's logistic and strategic choices.

ᴄᴦᵌᵏᴖ

Unsurprisingly, the information contained in the late Achaemenid sources does not turn the narrative of events upside down. At the same time these sources do throw light on the various lands of the empire, which are now becoming ever better known, and on the broad context in which Alexander

[78] Cf. Briant, *Rois, tributs et paysans*: 230–33; 247–48, 314–16; Briant, "Colonizazzione ellenistica e popolazione locale," in S. Settis, ed., *I Greci* II/2, Florence 1999: 309–33.

[79] See most recently, H.-P. Francfort and O. Lecomte, "Irrigation et société en Asie Centrale des origines à l'époque achéménide," *Annales HSS* 57/3 (2002): 625–63.

[80] On the fodder reserves in the empire, see the texts cited in Briant, "Empire of Darius," in B20 (2009): 155, n. 65.

conducted his military and organizational enterprises between 334 and 323. The observations and comments above lead us directly to the question, which has long been debated, of the continuities vs. changes from the Achaemenid to the Hellenistic period, including the ancillary question of the specific role played by Alexander, whether knowingly or not, in this process. In 1979, I tried to make an assessment and to suggest some directions for future research. I concluded that, in this respect, Alexander's reign could be regarded as an integral part of the history of the Middle East as initiated by the conquests of Cyrus and Cambyses. I ended with the following sentence:

> Was he the first of a long line of Hellenistic rulers? Of course! But I think that in the context of the history of the Near and Middle East in the first millennium, Alexander can also be considered as "the last of the Achaemenids."[81]

It is of course possible to question the validity of the expression "last of the Achaemenids."[82] But the problem is not in essence one of terminology, because, once the phrase is removed, the question of Achaemenid heritage and Macedonian innovation remains.

In the overall historiographical tradition, neither the underlying question nor the response I formulated thirty years ago is in any sense innovative. In this area, the influence of Rostovtzeff has been decisive, as has that of Aymard,

---

[81] "Des Achéménides aux rois hellénistiques. Continuités et ruptures. (Bilan et propositions)," = Briant, *Rois, tributs et paysans*: 291–30 (p. 330).

[82] R. Lane Fox, "Alexander the Great: 'Last of the Achaemenids'?" in C. Tuplin, ed., *Persian Responses: Political and Cultural Interaction with(in) the Achaemenid Empire*, Swansea 2007: 267–311; H.-U. Wiemer, "Alexander—der letzte Achämenide? Eroberungspolitik, lokale Eliten und altorientalische Traditionen im Jahr 323," *Historische Zeitschrift* 284 (2007): 281–309. Both articles deserve a thorough analysis; see some preliminary remarks in Briant, *Studi Ellenistici* XX (2008): 203, nn. 154, 162, 166; Briant, "The Empire of Darius," in B20 (2009), nn. 112, 122, 127.

Bikerman and Préaux, to name only three.[83] The problems are as old as the first thoughts on the Hellenistic period. When H. Bengtson in 1939 asked himself about the different views put forward by Tarn (B2: XII) and Berve (B2: VI) on the question of "universal brotherhood" (*Weltverbrüderung*), he could, with no need for justification, refer to "the question so often raised in recent years whether Alexander acted (or not) as a successor to the Achaemenids" (A1: 171). Nowadays, the continuity between Alexander and the Achaemenid model is often spoken of as if it were obvious, even though we, of course, question the nature and depth of that heritage. In 1992, Édouard Will reproached the author (H. Gehrke) of a book on the Hellenistic period for having neglected this aspect of the topic. His criticism is worth citing here:

> I must express a reservation which, beyond Alexander, affects the whole book: the object of the conquest itself, by which I mean the Persian empire, appears here in a somewhat ghostly fashion. But can we understand Alexander's empire and the subsequent Hellenistic empires of the Orient, without a reasonable understanding (however limited that may be) of the Achaemenid empire? . . . The slightness of the eastern substratum of the Hellenistic world leaves us craving more. . . . Recent studies have made us reevaluate our image of the Achaemenid empire, which offered in many respects the best global solution to the complex problems of the ethnic and cultural mosaic of the pre-Islamic East. . . . Alexander will certainly have understood that his work could not last unless he made use of the Achaemenid model. (*Gnomon* 64/1 [1992]: 68–69.)[84]

---

[83] See Briant, "Michel Rostovtzeff et le passage du monde achéménide au monde hellénistique," *Studi Ellenistici* XX (2008): 137–54.

[84] See my comments in Briant, *History*: 1007; also Briant, *Rois, tributs et paysans*: 505 and n. 41.

I do not intend to reexamine now a topic that is the central theme of this entire book. To end, I would simply under-score my critical message to the historian: that new readings of the available documents, the corpus of material found in recent years, and the clearer formulation of problems should between them encourage us to write a different history of Alexander; and this will be a history not limited to the pe-riod bounded by the two fixed dates 336/4 and 323. Rather it will be a history dynamically integrated into the longer period of transition that is defined at its upper end by the reigns of Philip II and Artaxerxes III (c. 350), and its lower end by the establishment of the new Hellenistic kingdoms around the year 300.

Index of Toponyms

Abydos, 30
Aegean, 44
Afghanistan, 82, 154, 163
Aigai, 3, 4
Ai-Khanoum, 82
Aleppo, 12
Alexandria in Egypt, 11, 56, 82, 117, 136
Alexandria in the Caucasus, 21
Alexandria on the Jaxartes, 117
Alexandria on the Tigris, 117
Alexandropolis, 2
Amu Darya. *See* Oxus River
Arabia, 22, 40, 80, 87, 91, 95
Arachosia, 15, 94, 113–14
Aradus, 9, 48
Arbela, 13, 175
Areia, 14–15, 55, 58, 113–14, 180
Armant, 105
Armenia, 75, 87, 114
Aspendos, 8, 35–36
Assyria, 90
Atarneus, 1
Athens, 2, 5, 31, 33–34, 36, 46, 54, 80, 87, 136–37, 142

Babylon, 13, 22–23, 43, 67, 76, 91, 94–95, 102, 106–7, 113, 130, 132, 138, 175
Babylonia, xiii, xvi, 7, 22, 46–47, 69, 90–91, 93–94, 99–100, 104, 105, 106, 107, 110, 113, 115, 137, 175, 179, 180
Bactra, 123, 125, 178
Bactria, xvi, 14–15, 20–21, 42, 55, 59, 64, 82, 99, 112–15, 138, 178–80, 182
Balkans, 5
Bithynia, 75

Bucheum, 105
Byblus, 9, 48
Byzantium, 2

Cappadocia, 9, 47, 75
Caria, 3, 71
Carmania, 72, 94, 113
Caspian Sea, 87
Chaeronea, 2, 28, 29
Chios, 10, 78, 79
Cilicia, 7, 9, 31, 39, 45, 70, 99
Cophen, 21
Corinth, 3, 5, 28, 35
Cyprus, 39, 48, 76, 97
Cyrene, 76
Cyropolis, 57

Damascus, 9, 12
Danube, 5
Daskyleion, 32, 124
Drangiana, 14, 15, 113, 121

Ecbatana, 13, 43, 64, 110
Egypt, xiii, xvi, 10–11, 13, 39–40, 43, 70–71, 77, 99, 104–5, 107, 110, 114, 119, 136–37, 162, 175, 178
Elam, 20, 22, 26, 91
Elephantine, xiv, 10
Ephesos, 35
Epirus, 3
Eresos, 137
Euphrates River, 10, 12, 26, 30, 51–52, 54, 82, 84, 90–93, 95–96, 175, 178
Europe, xiv, 12–14, 30, 34, 39, 46–47, 77–78, 86, 135, 156, 170

Fahliyun, 14
Fars, 12

Gandhara, 88
Ganges River, 38
Gaugamela, 12–13, 34, 52, 105–7
Gaza, 10, 48, 58, 117
Gedrosia, 27, 60, 70, 94
Gibraltar, 39
Gordion, 8, 34, 46
Granicus River, 7–8, 32–34, 44, 54, 68

Halicarnassus, 8, 44–45
Halys River, 47, 51–52
Hellespontus, 24, 49, 142
Helmand Valley, 94
Hindu Kush, 66, 154
Hydaspes River, 20–21
Hyphasis River, 20–21, 38, 65, 118, 129
Hyrcania, 114

Iberia, 39
India, 14, 20–22, 37, 40, 59–60, 66, 73–74, 83, 85, 87, 94, 96, 99, 111, 114–15, 117–18, 125–26, 129, 163
Indus River, xiv, 20–21, 26, 37–38, 76, 84, 94, 96
Iranian Plateau, 12, 14, 113
Isaura, 71
Issus, 7, 9, 12, 46, 48, 51–53, 77, 99, 162, 176

Jaxartes River, 56–57, 61, 82

Kabul River, 21
Karnak, 104
Kelainai, 8
Khorassan, 15

Laranda, 71
Lesbos, 1, 8, 10, 46, 78, 137
Libya, 39
Luxor, 104
Lyceum, 87
Lycia, 8, 45, 48
Lydia, xvi, 138

Macedon, xiv, 8, 10, 21, 29, 36, 48, 63, 65–66, 88, 97, 99, 118, 120, 130, 132, 136, 142–43, 156–57, 166–70, 173, 179
Maracanda, 122
Media, 13–14, 58, 73, 83, 99, 113–14, 121, 126
Megalopolis, 13, 53–54
Memphis, 104
Mesopotamia, 92
Mieza, 1
Miletus, 7, 8, 9, 33, 44, 45
Mytilene, 1, 8, 46, 128

Naucratis, 70
Nile River, 40, 87

Olympia, 137
Opis, 66, 118, 129, 130, 131, 133, 134
Oxus River, 55

Pallacopas, 90, 175
Pamphylia, 8, 45
Paphlagonia, 47, 75
Parapamisadae, 15, 115–16, 126
Parthia, 15, 58, 113, 126, 180
Pasargadae, 13, 26, 109, 111, 129
Pattala, 96
Pella, 1, 167
Peloponnesus, 53–54
Perinthus, 31
Persepolis, 12–14, 26, 43, 54, 63, 107, 109–110, 112–13, 123, 166–67, 170–71, 181
Persia, 5, 12, 20, 28, 31, 108, 110–11, 127, 162, 166, 175, 181
Persian Gulf, 20–22, 37–38, 40, 82, 87, 89, 94–96
Pharos, 136
Phoenicia, 9–10, 39, 47–48, 76–77, 95, 97, 99, 117
Phrygia, 8, 32, 46–47, 50, 68, 75
Pisidia, 8
Plataea, 34
Polytimetus River, 57

Priene, 68
Punjab, 37

Red Sea, 40, 87
Rhodes, 48
Rome, 34

Salamis, 34
Samaria, 11, 12, 176
Samarkand, xiv, 57
Samos, 142
Sardis, 8, 43, 75, 97, 102–4, 113–14
Scythia, 20, 82
Sicily, 39
Sidon, 9, 48, 76
Sinope, 31, 47
Siphnos, 46, 53
Siwa, 10, 76, 104, 119–20
Sogdian Rock, 116
Sogdiana, 14, 20, 42, 55, 58–59, 64,
    82, 112, 114–15, 122, 182
Soli, 48
Sparta, 9, 10, 12, 34–36, 46–47, 53,
    79, 120

Susa, 13, 22, 26, 34, 43, 54, 68, 89, 91,
    94, 102, 113, 128–30
Susiana, 91, 99, 113
Swat, 88
Syr Darya, 57, 82
Syria, 9, 11–12, 39, 70, 77, 99, 176
Syro-Phoenicia, 45

Tarsus, 9, 43, 99
Taxila, 70, 118
Thapsacus, 95
Thebaid, 105
Thebes, 5, 36
Thrace, 31, 53
Tigris River, 10, 13, 26, 82, 84, 89,
    90–93, 96, 99, 130
Tripolis, 9
Troy, 26
Tylos/Bahrein, 88
Tyre, 7, 9, 10–11, 46–48, 51, 54,
    76–77, 99, 176

Zagros, 63, 81
Zeravshan River, 57

General Index

Abdalonymus, 76
Abulites, 91, 113
Achaeans, 53
Achilles, 25–26, 74
Ada, 71
Aeschines, 53
Agis, 9–10, 12–13, 34, 46, 47, 53, 54, 79, 110
Alexander the Great
—administrative measures of: 67–80
—campaigns and battles of: 7–23, 42–58, 177–82
—coinage of: 96–100, 162–65
—colonies and cities founded by: 52–54, 80–83, 116–19, 176
—divinization of: 135–38
—historiography of: xiii–xiv, 83–86, 87–93, 89, 153–62, 166–68, 171–74, 182–85, 150
—and Macedon: 1–5, 52–54, 88, 138, 144, 168–71; and his army: 42–44, 52–54, 58–66, 129–33; and his court: 73–75, 76–80, 119–26, 133–35; and the Greek cities: 5, 28–29, 33–36, 52–54, 79–80, 110, 176; and the Iranians: 101–38; and Persepolis: 107–111, 170–71
—plans of: 24–41, 44–48, 83–96
—sources: xv-xix, 38–40, 61–63, 145–49
—and the succession: 139–144, 177–78
Alexander the Molossian, 3
Amminapes, 114
Amphoteros, 54
Amun, 11, 104, 119–20, 136, 162
Amyntas, 114
Anaxicrates, 87
Andromachus, 11

Andronicus, 48
Androsthenes, 87
Antigonus the One-Eyed, 8, 47
Antipater, 2, 13, 53–54, 78–80, 110, 132, 142
Apame, 129
Apelles, 135
Apis, 104
Archias, 87
Argead, 143, 166
Ariarathes, 75
Aristobulus, 61
Aristotle, 1–2, 87, 123
Arrian, xvi–xviii, 1, 7, 26, 39, 45–46, 50, 56–57, 60–61, 65, 68, 72–73, 82, 88–90, 92, 95, 103, 105, 108–9, 117, 123, 127, 129, 138
Arsakes, 58, 114
Arsites, 32, 50–51
Artabazus, 114, 129–30, 143
Artaxerxes II, 46
Artaxerxes III, 128, 167, 185
Artaxerxes IV, 167
Aspates, 113
Aspendians, 36
Athena, 33, 99
Athenaeus, 9
Athenians, 2
Atropates, 113, 126, 129
Attalus, 30
Auramazda, 124
Autophradates, 46, 48, 53, 113–14

Bagoas, xviii
Bagophanes, 105
Balakros, 47, 71
Barsine, 143
Batis, 48

Bel, 106
Bessos, 14–15, 55, 58, 112–13, 175,
    178–80
Bouchis, 105

Callisthenes, xv, 2, 87, 119, 123–25
Cambyses, 23, 104, 183
Carthaginians, 39
Chares, 128
Charidemos, 5
Chians, 79
Cleander, 73, 126
Cleomenes, 70, 136
Cleopatra, 3
Cossaeans, 22, 63, 81
Craterus, 94, 121
Cyrus, 23, 102, 105, 111–12, 129, 141,
    183

Darius I, 37, 40, 97, 104
Darius III, xiii–xiv, xvi–xviii, 8–10,
    12–14, 22–23, 28, 30, 32, 42–55, 59,
    63, 68–69, 102–3, 105, 107, 109,
    111–12, 128, 141, 162, 168, 170,
    172, 175–76, 178–79
Demades, 137
Demaratus, 3
Demosthenes, 137
Diodorus, xvii–xviii, 38, 50–51, 60,
    62, 69, 76, 80, 108, 111, 142
Dionysos, 25, 26, 37
Doloaspis, 70
Drypetis, 128

Egyptians, 120
Eleans, 53
Enylus, 48
Eudamus, 70
Eumenes, 74
Euripides, 122

Gerostratus, 48

Harpalus, 3, 74–75, 77, 80
Hegelochos, 10

Hephaestion, 10, 21, 63, 74, 89, 121–
    22, 128, 136, 169
Heracleides, 87
Heracon, 126
Herakles, 25–26, 37, 39, 99, 136
Hermias, 1
Herodotus, 40, 181
Hieron, 87
Homer, 26
Hydarnes, 47
Hypereides, 137
Hystaspes, 130

Isocrates, 30–32, 118

Justin, xvii

Kalas, 32, 47
Khababash, 43
Kleitos, 15, 119, 122–23, 125
Koinos, 65
Koiranos, 77
Korragos, 53

Lacedaemonians, 33, 53
Leonidas, 1
Leonnatus, 60
Lycurgus, 137
Lydians, 103
Lysippos, 34, 135

Macedonians, 2, 7, 13, 20–21, 27, 31–
    33, 39, 44, 50, 56, 58–59, 63, 65–66,
    71, 80–81, 84, 88, 101, 113–15,
    117–35, 137–38, 144
Mallians, 60, 127
Mardians, 113
Massagetae, 57
Mazakes, 10–11, 104
Mazday/Mazaeus, xv, 91, 99, 105–6,
    113, 115, 130, 175
Memnon, 8, 30, 44–46, 50–51, 53–54
Menon, 87, 113–14
Mithrenes, 75, 87, 103, 113–14
Mithropastes, 47

Mousikanos, 83
Myrseloi, 68

Nabarzanes, 14, 113
Nearchus, 3, 40, 47, 94
Nicanor, 79, 137

Olympias, 1–3, 25, 169
Omphis, 21
Orontobates, 8, 45, 47
Oxathres, 113
Oxyartes, 55, 58, 114, 116, 126
Oxydracians, 60

Parmenion, 9, 15, 30, 32, 64–65, 109,
   121–22, 142, 176
Parysatis, 128
Pausanias, 3–4
Pedieis, 68
Peloponnesians, 54
Perdiccas, 1, 21, 39, 121, 176
Peukestas, 127, 130
Pharnabazus, 46, 48, 53
Philip Arrhidaeus, 3, 143
Philip II, 1–5, 28–31, 33, 39, 44, 121–
   22, 131, 136, 143–44, 159, 167–70,
   173, 185
Philotas, 15, 119–22, 170
Philoxenos, 77–78
Phrataphernes, 113, 126
Pixodarus, 3–4
Plutarch, xvii–xviii, 3–4, 62–63, 85–
   86, 101–2, 136
Polybius, 28–29
Poros, 20–22, 38, 60, 76, 163

Proteus, 48
Ps.-Aristotle, 69, 71, 181
Ptolemy, 3, 60–61, 163, 165
Pyrgoteles, 135–36

Quintus Curtius, xvii–xviii, 9, 11, 51,
   59, 63, 108, 111, 115, 123, 143, 176

Roxane, 20, 114, 116, 123, 128, 130, 143

Sacae, 57
Sardians, 103
Satibarzanes, 15, 55, 58, 113–14
Scylax, 40
Scythians, 56, 57
Sitalces, 73, 126
Spitamenes, 15, 55–57, 59, 128
Stasanor, 114
Stateira, 128
Strabo, 89–90, 95
Straton, 76

Tapurians, 113
Taxiles, 21, 70, 76
Thais, 109
Theophrastus, 87, 88
Thracians, 2, 5
Tiridates, 109

Uxians, 13, 81

Xenophon, 62, 67, 73
Xerxes, 34, 106

Zeus, 99, 120, 136–137, 163

CPSIA information can be obtained
at www.ICGtesting.com
Printed in the USA
JSRC040030251121
R11311600001B/R113116PG20658JSX00001B/1